# DEADLY DISEASES AND EPIDEMICS

# TUBERCULOSIS

D0126654

# DEADLY DISEASES AND EPIDEMICS

Anthrax

Cholera

Influenza

Polio

Syphilis

Tuberculosis

# DEADLY DISEASES AND EPIDEMICS

# TUBERCULOSIS

## Kim R. Finer

CONSULTING EDITOR
**I. Edward Alcamo**
Distinguished Teaching Professor of Microbiology,
SUNY Farmingdale

FOREWORD BY
**David Heymann**
World Health Organization

**CHELSEA HOUSE**
P U B L I S H E R S
A Haights Cross Communications Company

**Philadelphia**

## Dedication

We dedicate the books in the DEADLY DISEASES AND EPIDEMICS series to Ed Alcamo, whose wit, charm, intelligence, and commitment to biology education were second to none.

## CHELSEA HOUSE PUBLISHERS

VP, NEW PRODUCT DEVELOPMENT  Sally Cheney
DIRECTOR OF PRODUCTION  Kim Shinners
CREATIVE MANAGER  Takeshi Takahashi
MANUFACTURING MANAGER  Diann Grasse

## Staff for Tuberculosis

ASSOCIATE EDITOR  Beth Reger
ASSISTANT EDITOR  Kate Sullivan
PRODUCTION EDITOR  Jamie Winkler
PHOTO EDITOR  Sarah Bloom
SERIES DESIGNER  Terry Mallon
COVER DESIGNER  Takeshi Takahashi
LAYOUT  21st Century Publishing and Communications, Inc.

A Haights Cross Communications 🜊 Company

http://www.chelseahouse.com

First Printing

1  3  5  7  9  8  6  4  2

Library of Congress Cataloging-in-Publication Data

Finer, Kim Renee, 1956–
    Tuberculosis / Kim Finer.
        v. cm.—(Deadly diseases and epidemics)
Includes index.
Contents: Tuberculosis throughout time—Robert Koch, Selman Waksman, and the near defeat of tuberculosis—The tuberculosis bacterium—Consumption: what happens once you become infected—Transmission from organism to organism—The immune response to tuberculosis infection—Screening for and diagnosis of tuberculosis—The BCG vaccine—Treatment of tuberculosis I: sanatoriums and early drug treatments—Treatment of tuberculosis II: modern drug therapy—The human immunodeficiency virus and tuberculosis.
    ISBN 0-7910-7309-2
    1. Tuberculosis—Juvenile literature. [1. Tuberculosis. 2. Diseases.] I. Title. II. Series.
RC311.1 .F54 2003
616.9'95—dc21

                                                    2002155988

# Table of Contents

**Foreword**
David Heymann, World Health Organization                    6

1.  Tuberculosis Throughout Time                    8

2.  Robert Koch, Selman Waksman, and
    the Near Defeat of Tuberculosis                 18

3.  The Tuberculosis Bacterium                      24

4.  Consumption: What Happens
    Once You Become Infected                        32

5.  Transmission from Organism to Organism          38

6.  The Immune Response to Tuberculosis Infection   46

7.  Screening for and Diagnosis of Tuberculosis     52

8.  The BCG Vaccine                                 62

9.  Treatment of Tuberculosis I:
    Sanatoriums and Early Drug Treatments           70

10. Treatment of Tuberculosis II:
    Modern Drug Therapy                             80

11. The Human Immunodeficiency
    Virus and Tuberculosis                          90


Glossary                                            98

Further Reading                                     102

Websites                                            104

Index                                               106

# Foreword

In the 1960s, infectious diseases—which had terrorized generations—were tamed. Building on a century of discoveries, the leading killers of Americans both young and old were being prevented with new vaccines or cured with new medicines. The risk of death from pneumonia, tuberculosis, meningitis, influenza, whooping cough, and diphtheria declined dramatically. New vaccines lifted the fear that summer would bring polio, and a global campaign was approaching the global eradication of smallpox. New pesticides like DDT cleared mosquitoes from homes and fields, thus reducing the incidence of malaria which was present in the southern United States and a leading killer of children worldwide. New technologies produced safe drinking water and removed the risk of cholera and other water-borne diseases. Science seemed unstoppable. Disease seemed destined to almost disappear.

But the euphoria of the 1960s has evaporated.

Microbes fight back. Those causing diseases like TB and malaria evolved resistance to cheap and effective drugs. The mosquito evolved the ability to defuse pesticides. New diseases emerged, including AIDS, Legionnaires, and Lyme disease. And diseases which haven't been seen in decades re-emerge, as the hantavirus did in the Navajo Nation in 1993. Technology itself actually created new health risks. The global transportation network, for example, meant that diseases like West Nile virus could spread beyond isolated regions in distant countries and quickly become global threats. Even modern public health protections sometimes failed, as they did in Milwaukee, Wisconsin in 1993 which resulted in 400,000 cases of the digestive system illness cryptosporidiosis. And, more recently, the threat from smallpox, a disease completely eradicated, has returned along with other potential bioterrorism weapons such as anthrax.

The lesson is that the fight against infectious diseases will never end.

In this constant struggle against disease, we as individuals have a weapon that does not require vaccines or drugs, the warehouse of knowledge. We learn from the history of science that "modern" beliefs can be wrong. In this series of books, for example, you will learn that diseases like syphilis were once thought to be caused by eating potatoes. The invention of the microscope set science on the right path. There are more positive lessons from history. For example, smallpox was eliminated by vaccinating everyone who had come in contact with an infected person. This "ring" approach to controlling smallpox is still the preferred method for confronting a smallpox outbreak should the disease be intentionally reintroduced.

At the same time, we are constantly adding new drugs, new vaccines and new information to the warehouse. Recently, the entire human genome was decoded. So too was the genome of the parasite that causes malaria. Perhaps by looking at the microbe and the victim through the lens of genetics we will to be able to discover new ways of fighting malaria, still the leading killer of children in many countries.

Because of the knowledge gained about such diseases as AIDS, entire new classes of anti-retroviral drugs have been developed. But resistance to all these drugs has already been detected, so we know that AIDS drug development must continue.

Education, experimentation, and the discoveries which grow out of them are the best tools to protect health. Opening this book may put you on the path of discovery. I hope so, because new vaccines, new antibiotics, new technologies and, most importantly, new scientists are needed now more than ever if we are to remain on the winning side of this struggle with microbes.

David Heymann
Executive Director
Communicable Diseases Section
World Health Organization
Geneva, Switzerland

# 1

# Tuberculosis Throughout Time

Fredric Chopin, Edgar Allan Poe, Eleanor Roosevelt, Charlotte Brontë, John Keats, Henry David Thoreau, King Edward IV, Doc Holliday— the list of the rich, famous, and infamous who became victims of tuberculosis is long and recognizable. Writers, politicians, scientists, poets—all segments of society were affected. Even today tuberculosis remains a public health threat. Nearly one-third of the world's population is currently infected, approximately eight million people will become newly infected this year, and two million people will die annually from the disease (Figure 1.1).

Tuberculosis was first described in ancient times. Scientists believe that the disease established itself firmly in human populations about the time humans transitioned from nomadic tribes to settled, agriculturally-based societies (8000 B.C.). These settlements provided sufficiently large groups through which the disease-causing microbes could find susceptible hosts.

## EVIDENCE OF TUBERCULOSIS IN EGYPT

The earliest archeological evidence of tuberculosis comes from ancient Egypt. Bones of Egyptian mummies dating from 2400 B.C. show evidence of decay caused by **Mycobacterium tuberculosis**, the bacterium that causes the disease tuberculosis. Many of these remains show erosion and fusion of the vertebrae, a result of infection by the organism (Figure 1.2). Tubercle bacilli have also been identified in bones dated to the period. The spinal form of tuberculosis, called **Potts Disease**, appears to

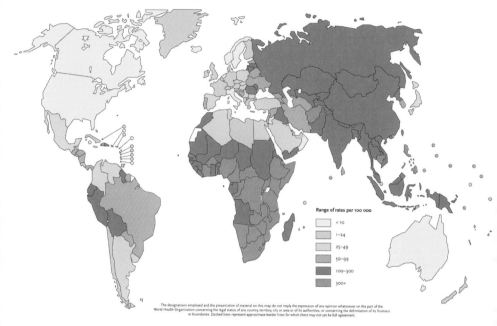

Range of rates per 100 000

- < 10
- 1–24
- 25–49
- 50–99
- 100–300
- 300+

The designations employed and the presentation of material on this map do not imply the expression of any opinion whatsoever on the part of the World Health Organization concerning the legal status of any country, territory, city or area or of its authorities, or concerning the delimitation of its frontiers or boundaries. Dashed lines represent approximate border lines for which there may not yet be full agreement.

**Figure 1.1** Tuberculosis occurs throughout the world, to varying degrees. As can be inferred from the map above, more cases of the disease occur in the less-industrialized countries. In the year 2000, the United States, Canada, and Australia had fewer than ten reported cases per 100,000 individuals, while much of sub-Saharan Africa reported more than 300 cases per 100,000 individuals.

have been particularly common in ancient Egypt. Depictions of hunched-back slaves as well as nobles are recognized in Egyptian art as far back as 3000 B.C.

Descriptions of typical signs and symptoms associated with tuberculosis which include the coughing of blood, fevers, night sweats, and weight loss or wasting, can be found in ancient writings. Clearly, people of the time recognized this malady as an evil, for which neither priests nor gods could offer a cure.

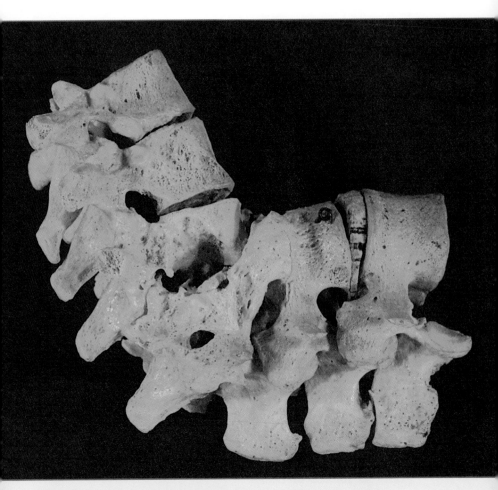

**Figure 1.2** When Mycobacterium tuberculosis infects the spinal column, the bones begin to disintegrate. The disease destroys the bone, forming holes. This can cause stiffness, pain, tenderness, and even paralysis. The vertebrae in the picture above have been infected with tubercle bacilli. Notice the holes in the bone where the disease has destroyed the tissue.

### GREEK AND ROMAN INTEREST IN TUBERCULOSIS

The ancient Greeks had a genuine interest in medicine which they considered a science rather than in the realm of religion, as many cultures believed. Greek scholars wrote on many medical subjects including tuberculosis. The Greeks called tuberculosis "**phthisis**" (tiz' is). Although a clear derivation and definition of the word is not generally agreed upon, it may come from the ancient Greek word that means "to waste" or "consume." **Consumption** is the term used in the Old Testament of the Bible to describe tuberculosis, and both terms, phthisis and consumption, were used by the Greeks, Romans, Hebrews, and eventually Europeans, to describe tuberculosis through the early 1900s.

The Greek physician Hippocrates mentioned tuberculosis in many of his writings and is believed to have first used the word phthisis to describe the disease. Hippocrates speculated that the disease was caused by growths that he observed in the lungs. His writings also suggest that he associated tuberculosis of the spine with the same disease occurring in the lungs.

Although best known as a famous Greek philosopher, Plato was also trained as a physician. Plato provided a practical, if not ethical, warning against the treatment of tuberculosis. He advised that treating the disease "was of no advantage to themselves or to the State" because the patient would most likely die. Certainly Plato's warning stemmed from the fact that the disease would probably result in death, and there was, therefore, no sense trying to treat it.

Around A.D. 162, the Greek physician, **Galen** (Figure 1.3), a favorite of the Roman Emperor Marcus Aurelius, practiced medicine in Rome. Galen, an astute observer who performed autopsies on animals and wrote anatomy texts, guessed that tuberculosis might be infectious. He prescribed a treatment for the disease consisting of fresh milk, open air, sea breezes, and dry mountainous places. Because the infectious nature of the disease remained a mystery, this prescription would be the best that medicine had to offer for the treatment of tuberculosis for almost the next 1700 years!

**Figure 1.3** Although originally from Greece, Claude Galien (Galen), pictured above, practiced medicine in Rome. He had a keen interest in the workings of the human body. In addition to his research in tuberculosis, he spent a great deal of his professional life studying the circulatory system.

## THE MIDDLE AGES

The years that followed the great Roman Empire included very little writing about, or interest in, science or medicine. Religious thought dominated this period known as the Dark Ages, and religious zealots discouraged inquiry or scientific explanation of natural events. Consequently, little is known of the extent or incidence of tuberculosis during this time. The one form of tuberculosis we do know about during medieval times was an infliction known as **scrofula** (skräf' yoo la). Scrofula is the name given to tuberculosis of the lymph nodes. When infected, these glands become enlarged and rubbery to the touch. Early monarchs, who believed they ruled through divine power, claimed the power to heal scrofula by touch. King Edward I of England (reigned 1272–1307) is said to have touched 533 afflicted subjects in a single month in 1277, and in the 1600s, King Henry VII began the practice of giving a gold angel or amulet to those he touched. Shakespeare, the great English playwright, described this ritual to cure scrofula in his play *Macbeth.*

> Tis called the Evil:
> A most miraculous work in this good king;
> Which often since my here-remain in England
> I have seen him do. How he solicits heaven,
> Himself best knows; but strangely visited people,
> All swoln and ulcerous, pitiful to the eye,
> The mere despair of surgery, he cures;
> Hanging a golden stamp about their necks,
> Put on with holy prayers; and 'tis spoken ,
> To the succeeding royalty he leaves
> The healing benediction.
>
> *Macbeth, IV, iii, 146*

As Europe emerged from the Dark Ages, there was a renaissance of not only art but also medicine and science. This interest in science coincided with the tuberculosis epidemic in Europe that began in the early 1600s and continued over the next two centuries. Increased population centers, as well as poverty, contributed to the growing number of cases. Tuberculosis became known as the Great White Death and was almost as feared as the Black Death or bubonic plague of earlier times.

## TUBERCULOSIS IN THE AMERICAS

Some historians have suggested that along with a few other plagues, Columbus brought tuberculosis to the new world. However, in 1994 scientists from Minnesota dispelled that rumor. Using sophisticated molecular techniques, DNA from *Mycobacterium tuberculosis* was discovered in fossilized remains of a woman in her forties who lived with, but apparently did not die from, tuberculosis. This woman lived in an arid desert region of Peru almost 400 years before Columbus discovered America. From this evidence one can conclude that tuberculosis was present in the Americas before Columbus ever set foot in the region.

Although we have evidence that tuberculosis was present in the Americas prior to the arrival of European settlers, Native Americans of North and South America had little trouble with tuberculosis, in part due to the fact that there were few major population centers. Tuberculosis organisms which lack a large number of susceptible hosts living close together fail to establish disease in a population.

Tuberculosis remained a rare disease among native North Americans well into the 1800s, and would only become a problem when these indigenous people were forced to settle on reservations, live in barracks, or reside in prison camps. In these settings, contacts with European Americans became more frequent, and the crowding promoted airborne transmission of the bacterium. In 1886, the death rate for Native Americans from tuberculosis was 90 per 1000 individuals, a figure ten times greater than the highest death rate in Europe in the 1600s!

## THE DISEASE ROMANTICIZED

While tuberculosis was feared throughout the 1600s, it was romanticized during the 1700s, 1800s, and early 1900s. The gaunt, fragile, vulnerable look of consumption became fashionable. It was considered glamorous to look sickly. Camille

Saint-Säens, a famous composer of the time, wrote in 1913 that "it was fashionable to be pale and drained." The dying young person was often thought to possess a romantic personality and have creative gifts. This was especially true among those in literature and the arts. The poet Percy Shelly wrote to fellow poet John Keats, "this consumption is a disease particularly fond of people who write such good verses as you have done." John Keats, who studied medicine and was torn between writing poetry and practicing medicine, was very familiar with tuberculosis. His mother died of the disease when Keats was 14 years old, and his brother later developed tuberculosis. In the summer of 1829, Keats noticed blood when he coughed deeply. He immediately recognized this sign as a death warrant and was dead one year later.

Robert Louis Stevenson, another famous writer of the time (*Treasure Island, Dr. Jekyll and Mr. Hyde, Kidnapped*), developed tuberculosis as a child, but the course of his disease contrasted greatly with that of Keats. Beginning at the age of 25, Stevenson traveled around the world trying to find a climate where he would be free of his tuberculosis symptoms. After spending time in France and Switzerland, he eventually became a patient at Edwards Trudeau's **sanatorium** in Saranac Lake, New York (sanatoriums will be discussed in more detail in Chapter 9). Although Stevenson had tuberculosis throughout his adult life, he was not overly weakened by the disease. He continued to travel and write until he died at the age of 44 of a condition unrelated to his tuberculosis.

In the 1700s, many causes were attributed to tuberculosis: heredity (the Brontë family provided excellent evidence for this theory), unfavorable climate, laziness, depression, and lack of air and light. The most famous pathologist of the late 1800s, Rudolf Virchow, refused to believe tuberculosis was infectious. However, other scientists did not share this view. Those scientists were carrying out experiments and making observations that would eventually reveal the cause of the disease.

## DID YOU KNOW?

The literary Brontë family was hit particularly hard by tuberculosis. The Reverend Patrick Brontë and his wife Marie had six children. Marie died at age 38 shortly after the birth of her last child from childbed fever, a puzzling condition of the 1800s that resulted in the death of a significant number of women who had recently given birth (although she may also have had tuberculosis). Reverend Brontë had a chronic cough that was probably caused by tuberculosis. Maria, the oldest Brontë daughter died from tuberculosis at age 12, and her sister Elizabeth died one month later at age 11. Two years later, Branwell, the Brontë's only son, died at age 25 with sister Emily (author of *Wuthering Heights*) dying a few months later at the age of 30. Anne died at age 29, five months after Emily, and Charlotte (author of *Jane Eyre*) died from tuberculosis at age 39. Amazingly, Reverend Brontë lived until the age of 85.

### THE TRUE NATURE OF THE DISEASE

In the early 1700s an English physician named Benjamin Marten wrote a book entitled *A New Theory of Consumption: More Especially of a Phthisis or Consumption of the Lungs*. In his book, Dr. Marten suggested that tuberculosis might be caused by the "wonderfully minute living creatures," or the animalcules described by Anton von Leeuwenhoek, inventor of a microscope able to view bacteria and fungi in 1676. Marten wrote his book 160 years before the bacterium was viewed and described by the German physician **Robert Koch**, and shown to be connected to disease. Unfortunately, the book went unnoticed by most scientists of Dr. Marten's day.

It was not until 1865 that a formal demonstration proving that tuberculosis could be transmitted was conducted. Jean-Antoine Villemin, a French physician, inoculated rabbits with pus and fluid from human and cattle tuberculosis lesions.

When he examined the lungs and lymph nodes of the dead rabbits he found tubercular lesions.

With the above descriptions and discoveries, the stage was set for learning the true cause of tuberculosis. Although the discipline of microbiology was in its infancy, the burgeoning interest in the study of microorganisms was about to provide information about the causes and even cures for many of the deadly diseases that had been plaguing humans since ancient times.

# 2

# Robert Koch, Selman Waksman, and the Near Defeat of Tuberculosis

Robert Koch (Figure 2.1) was born December 11, 1843, one of 13 children in Clausthal, Lower Saxony, Germany. As a young boy he had an interest in nature and spent much of his time collecting plants and insects. At the age of 19, Koch entered the University at Gottingen, Germany, where he was an outstanding student (although he was not a particularly good student before entering the university). While at the university, he won a research prize and published two scientific papers. He received his doctorate at the age of 23 and began practicing medicine at the Hamburg General Hospital. He later married his childhood sweetheart and went into private medical practice.

When war broke out between Germany and France in 1870, Koch tried to enlist in the army but was rejected because of his poor eyesight. Upon his second attempt at enlisting, he was accepted to serve as a doctor. Koch served in a battlefield hospital where his war experience impacted him greatly. He became very nationalistic, and violently anti-French (this would affect him later in his dealings with Louis Pasteur, the famous French microbiologist).

Following the war, Koch went back to his medical practice and also spent time conducting research in his laboratory. He was especially interested in the disease anthrax which is caused by the bacterium *Bacillus anthracis*. In his laboratory, he was able to culture the anthrax bacillus in liquid media and view the organism using the microscope his wife had purchased for him as a birthday present. Koch was also able to observe the development of spores from the anthrax bacilli, thereby linking the bacillus to the spores found in the

**Figure 2.1** Robert Koch is one of the founders of the discipline of microbiology. He studied anthrax, cholera, and tuberculosis, and attempted to create a tuberculosis vaccine. Koch also developed a set of rules for all scientists to follow to identify the microorganisms that produced specific diseases. Known as **Koch's postulates**, they are still a fundamental aspect of microbiology today. Koch is pictured here at the age of 62, as he appeared in 1905 in his Nobel Prize photograph.

blood of anthrax-infected animals. Koch presented his research in April 1876 to a group from the Institute of Plant Science in Breslau. The audience of scientists was very impressed; Koch had clearly established that bacteria cause the disease anthrax.

Ferdinand Cohn, Director of the Institute of Plant Science, was so impressed with Koch's research that he was able to secure a position for the young scientist at the Imperial Health Office in Berlin. During his first year in Berlin, Koch was a very busy man; he developed the steam method of sterilization, he showed that the bacteria streptococci and staphylococci could cause wound infections, he was the first scientist to use an oil immersion lens to view bacteria, and he developed a solid culture medium on which to grow pure cultures of bacteria.

Koch began his work on tuberculosis in 1881. He was assisted in the laboratory by Freidrich Loeffler and Georg Gaffky. Both men would later go on to make famous discoveries themselves. After only seven months of work, Koch presented his research on tuberculosis at the monthly meeting of the Berlin Physiological Society. At that meeting, Koch presented proof that *Mycobacterium tuberculosis* (*Bacillus tuberculosis* was the name used by Koch) was the cause of the disease tuberculosis. In his presentation, Koch put forth the steps which he used to arrive at his conclusions. These steps, known as Koch's postulates, are still used today to establish that a particular bacterium causes a specific disease.

Although Koch turned his attention for a brief time to cholera, he continued to search for a cure for tuberculosis. Robert Koch was a great scientist, but his personal pride, a tendency towards not sharing experimental results with other scientists, and perhaps a sense of German nationalism caused an unfortunate blunder regarding the development of a tuberculosis vaccine.

Under great pressure from the German government to prove its country's intellectual superiority, Koch publicly stated in 1890 that he had developed a method for producing resistance against the tuberculosis bacterium, a vaccine called **tuberculin**. In the words of Koch he had "found substances that halted the

## MAKING THEIR OWN MARK

Koch's first two assistants, Fredrich Loeffler and Georg Gaffky went on to become famous for their own discoveries. Loeffler discovered the cause of diphtheria, and Gaffky described the cause of cholera. The Gaffky scale is used today to describe the number of tubercle bacilli in the sputum of tuberculosis patients.

growth of tuberculosis bacilli not only in test tubes, but also in animal bodies."[1] Unfortunately, the vaccine which had been tested only in guinea pigs produced serious and sometimes deadly side effects in humans. When data ultimately showed the vaccine to be ineffective, Koch's reputation was somewhat tarnished. Nonetheless, Koch still was awarded the Nobel Prize in medicine in 1905 for his studies on tuberculosis.

Following retirement as the Director of the Institute for Infectious Disease in Berlin, Koch and his wife traveled extensively. Robert Koch died in 1910 at the age of 66 from a heart attack.

## KOCH'S POSTULATES

Although technology has increased the speed at which we can detect or diagnose disease, some things have not changed. Today, 120 years after Koch first described them, the set of steps known as Koch's postulates are still used to determine that a particular organism causes a particular disease. The steps are as follows:

1. Isolation of the bacterium from sick and dying animals.

2. Growth and identification of the organism in the laboratory.

3. Reproduction of the disease in a laboratory animal.

4. Isolation of the organisms from the laboratory animal in which the disease was reproduced and careful comparison to determine a "match" with the original disease causing bacterium.

### THE MAGIC BULLET

While the most widely prescribed treatment for tuberculosis, even after Koch's discovery, remained the advice of Galen (rest, sea travel, and fresh air), governments and the public began to mobilize their efforts to defeat the disease. In 1892, the first

---

1. D.S. Burke, "Of Postulates and Peccadilloes: Robert Koch and vaccine (tuberculin) therapy for tuberculosis," *Vaccine* 11 (1993): 795–804.

local tuberculosis association was formed in Philadelphia. The Christmas Seal program, initially sponsored by the Red Cross and taken over by the National Tuberculosis Association in 1920, began to raise a great deal of money to fund tuberculosis research. X-rays, discovered in 1895 by William Roentgen, were being used to rapidly screen millions of Americans for lung lesions, while local regulations against spitting, and/or coughing in public were enforced. The **BCG** vaccine (described in detail in Chapter 8) against tuberculosis was being used in Europe, although its effectiveness was a point of debate.

**Selman Waksman** (Figure 2.2) was born in 1888 in Odessa, Ukraine. As a young man he moved to the United States and attended Rutgers University in New Jersey where he studied a group of soil bacteria called actinomycetes. He eventually earned his Ph.D. and became a recognized expert in the field of soil microbiology. With the advent of World War II, Waksman decided to pursue research in the area of **antibiotics**, substances produced by one microorganism that can inhibit the growth of, or kill, other microorganisms. Waksman's interest in antibiotics combined with his knowledge of actinomycetes culminated in the isolation of the antibiotic **streptomycin** (strep' tōmī' sin), a product of the soil actinomycete, *Streptomyces griseus* in 1943.

Streptomycin was first used in humans in 1944 to treat a young woman dying of tuberculosis. At first, a crude preparation was used to treat her disease, and she failed to improve. In early 1945, a more purified form of the antibiotic became available for use. The new preparation was administered to the woman described above. She immediately began to get better. The number of tubercle bacilli in her **sputum** decreased and one of her lungs showed marked improvement. A follow-up exam of the patient ten years later showed that the disease had remained inactive as a result of the streptomycin treatment.

Initial hopes for streptomycin were somewhat dashed because the antibiotic produced side effects in some patients and did not destroy the organism in others. Even worse, in some patients, antibiotic resistant forms of the tubercle bacilli

**Figure 2.2** Selman Waksman, pictured here, first discovered the use of streptomycin as an antibiotic. Streptomycin was tested in a woman who was suffering from tuberculosis in 1944. Although the antibiotic was not a perfect solution, as it had some side effects and did not always cure the disease, it gave hope to tuberculosis patients and paved the way for future research.

began to emerge. Fortunately, more effective antibiotics with fewer side effects would soon become available including para-aminosalicylic acid in 1948, isoniazid in 1951, ethambutol in 1961, and rifampin in 1967.

With the use of antibiotics to treat tuberculosis, Galen's prescription was finally replaced. As a consequence, sanatoriums that had been established to treat tuberculosis suffers (Chapter 9) began to close. The impact of public health programs, and treating the disease with antibiotics produced a constant decline in the number of tuberculosis cases from 1959 until the mid-1980s. Yet even as we move into a new century, tuberculosis is still with us. The disease continues to present new public health challenges by targeting particular segments of the population and teaming with a relatively new disease, **Acquired Immune Deficiency Syndrome (AIDS)**.

# 3

# The Tuberculosis Bacterium

The disease tuberculosis can be caused by one of four different organisms belonging to the genus mycobacterium. *Mycobacterium bovis, Mycobacterium africanum, Mycobacterium microti,* and *Mycobacterium tuberculosis* are the four species that make up the tuberculosis complex. Of the four different organisms, **Mycobacterium tuberculosis** is the most common cause of tuberculosis in human beings. *Mycobacterium africanum* is usually found only in northwestern Africa, and **Mycobacterium bovis**, which causes disease in cattle, is now only a rare cause of human tuberculosis because it is usually destroyed during pasteurization of milk from cattle. All four organisms mentioned are very similar and almost indistinguishable in the laboratory. Only very minor biochemical and genetic differences separate members of the group.

## PHYSICAL CHARACTERISTICS

The organism *Mycobacterium tuberculosis* (my'-koh-bak-tee'-ree-um too'-ber-ku-lo-sis) is a slow-growing, long, slender, rod-shaped bacterium. The size of the bacillus falls within the range of 0.2-0.6µm x 1.0-10 µm (a µm equals one millionth of a meter). In body tissues, the organisms often form long-massed filaments of cells which are called **cords**. The capacity to form cords is related to the organism's **virulence**, or ability of the organism to cause disease.

Like all prokaryotic organisms, the tubercle bacillus is a simple cell. The bacterium is rod-shaped and surrounded by a multilayered cell wall containing mycolic acids. On the inside of the cell wall lies the cell membrane, a lipid bilayer that controls what goes into and out of the bacterium. Lipids are a broad group of organic compounds that do not generally dissolve in water. The best known lipids are fats. On the inside of the cell membrane is the cytoplasm which contains genetic material, ribosomes, vacuoles, and granules.

Tubercle bacilli do not form capsules, produce flagella, or form spores. They do not produce toxins or many of the other enzymes that are normally associated with the disease process. Although the tuberculosis bacterium has few, if any, of the virulence factors we normally associate with the ability to cause disease, it can still wreak havoc in a susceptible host.

The organism creates problems for the host, in part, because of the makeup of the cell wall. The organism has a cell wall that contains not only **peptidoglycan** (pep' tĭd ō gly kan), a complex carbohydrate, as do other bacteria, but also contains large wax-like lipids called **mycolic** (mīkol' ic) **acids**. The mycolic acids of mycobacteria are very large organic molecules containing anywhere from 60–90 carbons.

These lipids provide a layer which protects the organism from harsh chemicals, many antibiotics, and antibodies (protective proteins produced by the human host). The mycolic acid of the cell wall also aids in preventing digestion of the organisms by phagocytic cells. The ability to resist digestion allows the organisms to ultimately establish infection and cause disease.

Mycolic acids also make the bacteria resistant to drying. This allows the organism to survive for a long time in dried sputum. This characteristic of the organism poses an infection risk for the unsuspecting victim.

## STAINING CHARACTERISTICS
## OF MYCOBACTERIA

A very important tool in the classification of bacteria is the Gram stain. This staining method, discovered by Hans Christian Gram in 1884, separates most bacteria into one of two groups: Gram-negative bacteria or Gram-positive bacteria. Gram-positive bacteria have a cell wall composed of a thick layer of peptidoglycan. Gram-negative bacteria have cell walls composed of a thin layer of peptidoglycan and an additional layer called the outer membrane. When performing the Gram stain on mycobacteria, the primary stain will not wash out because of the mycolic acids present. Generally, organisms are considered Gram-positive if they retain the initial stain and color purple, and Gram

## DID YOU KNOW?

Hans Christian Joachim Gram was a Danish physician working in the morgue of a Berlin hospital in 1884 when he developed a method to stain bacteria found in infected lung tissue. This staining procedure, now known as the Gram stain, generally divides the world of bacteria into two groups: Gram-positive bacteria and Gram-negative bacteria. Following completion of the staining procedure, Gram-positive organisms will appear purple and Gram-negative organisms appear pink (or red). This staining distinction is based upon the fact that the two groups of bacteria have cell walls which are structurally and chemically different. Because of their mycolic acid layer, mycobacteria do not stain appropriately with the Gram stain; therefore, Paul Ehrlich, a pupil of Robert Koch's developed another stain to differentiate these organisms from others: the **acid-fast stain**. In this stain, the fuchsia-colored primary stain will not wash out even when using an acid-alcohol—thus the name "acid-fast." Organisms that are not acid-fast will appear blue which is the color of the counter stain.

negative if the initial stain washes out and the cell takes up the counterstain instead (usually safranin, which gives the bacteria a reddish-pink color). However, this stain does not work on mycobacteria due to the high lipid content of its cell wall.

Since the Gram stain will not work correctly on the mycobacteria, another stain, the **acid-fast stain**, is used to differentiate and visualize the organism. In the acid-fast stain (Figure 3.1), the primary dye will only be retained if the cell wall of the organism contains mycolic acids.

## CHARACTERISTICS OF
## MYCOBACTERIA IN CULTURE

*Mycobacterium tuberculosis* grows very slowly. One bacillus takes approximately 20 hours to divide, as opposed to *E. coli*, for example, which replicates approximately every 20 minutes. A colony of *Mycobacteria tuberculosis* will take several weeks to grow large enough to be seen on laboratory media. Some scientists suggest that the slow growth rate is due to the sluggish action of the organism's RNA polymerase, the enzyme responsible for transcribing DNA into RNA which will ultimately be translated into protein.

When grown in broth cultures, masses of bacilli form in a chain-like fashion on the surface of the media giving the appearance of dense mold-like layers. The genus name, mycobacterium, is derived from the Greek word *mykes,* which means fungal or mold-like.

It can be difficult to grow mycobacteria in the laboratory because the organisms will not grow on ordinary culture media. Special media containing egg yolk is often used to cultivate the bacilli. When grown at 35°–37°C on solid media, the organism will produce colonies in three to six weeks. These colonies are usually a buff or beige color and have a rough, dry, granular appearance (Figure 3.2).

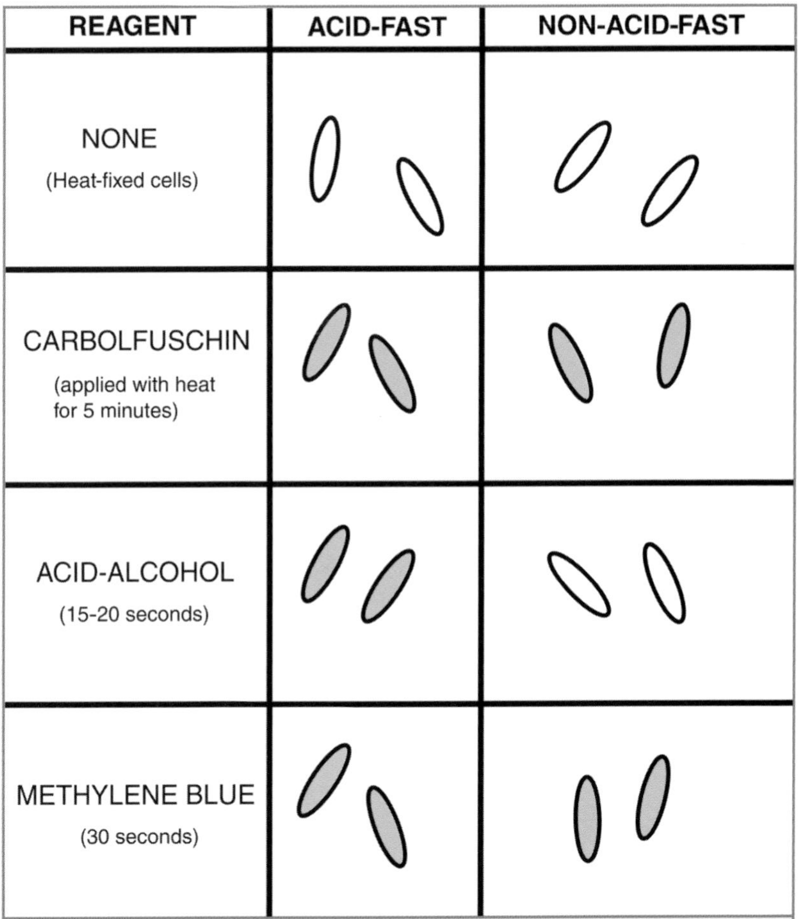

| REAGENT | ACID-FAST | NON-ACID-FAST |
|---------|-----------|---------------|
| NONE<br>(Heat-fixed cells) | | |
| CARBOLFUSCHIN<br>(applied with heat<br>for 5 minutes) | | |
| ACID-ALCOHOL<br>(15-20 seconds) | | |
| METHYLENE BLUE<br>(30 seconds) | | |

**Figure 3.1** The cell walls of some bacteria contain mycolic acids, which form a waxy layer around the cells. Due to this waxy layer, the cells are not suited for the Gram stain. The acid-fast stain is used instead. Carbolfuschin, a red dye, is applied to bacteria that have been smeared on a slide, and the slide is heated which allows the dye to penetrate the waxy layer of the cell wall. After the slide cools, it is washed with acid-alcohol which will remove the stain from any cells that do not contain mycolic acids. Methylene blue is applied as a counterstain. Cells that do not have the waxy layer will absorb the counterstain and appear blue. These cells are not acid-fast. Cells that appear red have retained only the original carbolfuschin stain and are considered acid-fast.

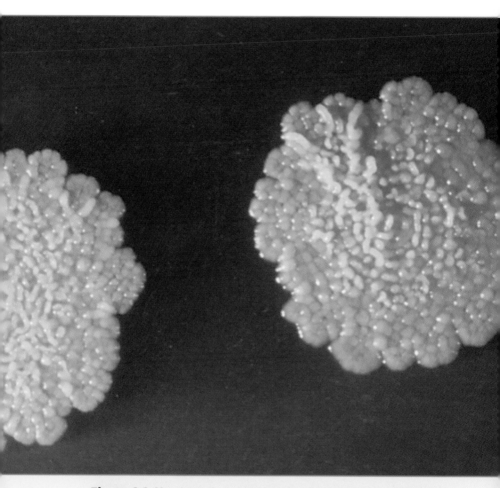

**Figure 3.2** *Mycobacterium tuberculosis* colonies grow very slowly, and can only be cultivated on special media. Cultures grown in broth have a fungus-like appearance. Cultures grown on solid media, shown here, have a beige-colored, dry, granular appearance. The tuberculosis bacteria require oxygen to grow and reproduce, which is one reason why the bacteria favor the lungs.

Most mycobacteria are strict aerobic organisms, meaning that they require oxygen to grow and reproduce. The oxygen requirement explains why the bacilli reproduce particularly well in the lungs.

## GENETICS OF
## THE ORGANISM

In 1996, The Institute for Genomic Research (abbreviated TIGR, and located in Rockville, Maryland) began sequencing the **genome** of a strain of *Mycobacterium tuberculosis* called "Oshkosh" or CDC-1515. The Oshkosh strain was originally isolated from a man who worked in a children's clothing factory. The strain was particularly contagious. Approximately 80 percent of the man's coworkers and social contacts were infected by this single individual.

Results from TIGR's sequencing efforts, as well as research at the Sanger Centre in England, indicate that the circular genome of *Mycobacterium tuberculosis* is composed of 4,403,765 base pairs (TIGR). These bases encode approximately 4,000 genes. Of those genes, 43 percent have known biological roles, 15 percent match genes from other species, and 42 percent have no current database match and probably represent unique genes.

Scientists are looking to these unique genes and their proteins as well as other genes for clues as to how the organism persists in the body and successfully outwits the host immune system. Several genes are now being investigated as potential drug or vaccine targets (Table 3.1). Of particular interest are those genes which enable the organism to survive inside the macrophage. These include genes for lipid metabolism, cell wall synthesis, and regulation of transcription.

**Table 3.1** Target genes for tuberculosis therapy and their functions

| GENE NAME | FUNCTION |
| --- | --- |
| *icl* | Gene which codes for an enzyme that makes fatty acids available for energy |
| *erp* | Gene that codes for proteins required for multiplication within the host phagocytic cells |
| *pcaA* | Gene that plays a role in the strength of the cell wall and ability to form cords |
| *sigF* | Regulatory gene which controls survival in tubercles |

# 4

# Consumption: What Happens Once You Become Infected

On a flight from Paris to New York in 1998, over 250 passengers inhaled and exhaled the same cabin air not knowing that one of them had a severe cough. During the course of the next few months, 12 individuals on the flight were diagnosed with tuberculosis. Were they victims infected by one individual during an eight-hour flight? What about the other 237 passengers and flight crew? Why didn't they become infected? Maybe some of them did—and they just didn't realize it.

### TUBERCULOSIS INFECTION

It may take as few as eight to ten tuberculosis bacilli to cause tuberculosis infection. Upon inhalation, the organisms contained in **droplet nuclei** (small droplets of sputum containing two-three bacilli) enter the body and make their way deep into the lungs where they will be ingested by special phagocytic cells called **macrophages**. Macrophages (Figure 4.1) are responsible for acting as sentinels to keep unwanted organisms out of the lower respiratory tract.

Following macrophage ingestion, the war between host and microorganism begins. The situation can have two possible outcomes depending upon the killing power of the host's macrophages and the ability of the organism to cause disease. Strong phagocytic cells may ingest and destroy the bacilli, preventing both infection and disease.

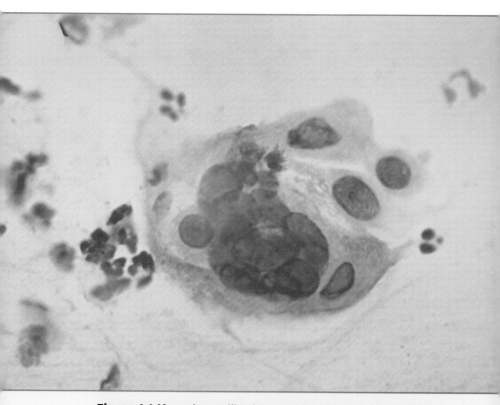

**Figure 4.1** Macrophages, like the one pictured here, are cells of the body's defense system. They act as soldiers to protect the body and attack foreign invaders. Macrophages are a type of phagocytic cell. Phagocyte means "eating cell" and these cells literally swallow the invading microorganism whole.

Alternately, the invading organisms may continue to live and even replicate inside the phagocytic cell. While inside the phagocytic cells, many organisms are carried to the lymph nodes. Lymph nodes are small glands found throughout the body that filter out harmful substances and produce **lymphocytes**. In the lymph nodes, the organisms may be destroyed or continue to grow and eventually **lyse**, or break open, the host phagocytic cells, thus gaining access to other parts of the body.

If the bacilli remain alive in the host's cells, one to four weeks after the initial infection the host's specific immune system will begin to mount an organized attack against the tuberculosis bacilli. Macrophages seek out and organize around the bacteria, forming large-multinucleated cells called "**giant cells**." Additional macrophages and other immune cells called lymphocytes begin to assemble and wall off the bacteria. The collection of immune cells, bacilli, and host cells forms a **tubercle** (too' ber kul, from the Latin word for knob or swelling).

These tubercles wall off and may hold the organism in check throughout the rest of the infected person's life. In some infected individuals, the tubercle may decay due to the release of enzymes by the bacteria and host cells. This decay results in soft, cheesy-like ooze called **caseous exudate**,

## DID YOU KNOW?

There are many different types of cells which function in the immune response. Phagocytic cells, or "cells that eat," are immune cells which are responsible for ingesting and destroying anything the body perceives as "non-self." Phagocytic cells come in one of two types: those that have granules in their cytoplasm (granulocytes) and those that do not (agranulocytes). A macrophage is a type of agranulocyte that is found in the tissues and is highly efficient at eliminating foreign materials from the body. Although macrophages are found in all tissues, they are present in large numbers in the lungs, liver, spleen, and lymph nodes. Lymphocytes are another group of immune cells. Lymphocytes (B cells and T cells) have no phagocytic capability, but play major roles in the specific immune response. B cells produce antibodies and T cells directly kill or release compounds that ultimately lead to the death of the invading microorganisms.

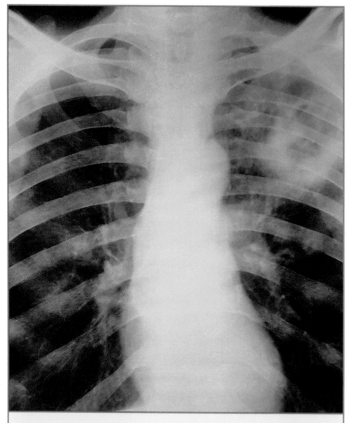

**Figure 4.2** Tubercles can effectively contain the bacillus, or they can decay into an oozy lesion. These lesions can calcify and form deposits within the lungs, containing the infection once more. These calcifications can be seen in an X-ray. The chest X-ray pictured here shows tubercle calcifications in the upper left area of the lung (upper right portion of the X-ray). These spots represent formerly active foci of *Mycobacterium tuberculosis* infection.

(kā' sē ∂s eks' yŏŏ dāt) in the center of the lesion. This lesion may become calcified and heal—again halting the infection and containing the organisms. The calcified tubercles are sometimes visible on an X-ray of an infected person's chest (Figure 4.2).

The entire story might end at this stage with no further complications. People who have the tuberculosis *infection* just described do not feel sick, have no symptoms, and are not infectious. They have what is often described as **latent tuberculosis**. Individuals with latent tuberculosis will have a positive result from a tuberculosis test and can develop tuberculosis later in life (reactivation) if their immune system becomes weak.

## TUBERCULOSIS DISEASE

If the tubercle ruptures and releases organisms into either the blood stream or the bronchi, infected material may spread throughout the body or further into the lungs. When the organism spreads throughout the body, it can produce small yellow nodules one to two millimeters in diameter. This form of disseminated tuberculosis is often called **miliary** (mil' ē er' ē) **tuberculosis** because the nodules resemble the grain millet.

The unchecked replication and dissemination of tuberculosis bacilli is indicative of tuberculosis *disease*. Tuberculosis disease occurs in about ten percent of individuals who have the tuberculosis infection. Tuberculosis disease is usually the result of a weakened immune system which can no longer contain the invading organisms.

Physical signs that someone has the disease include: a severe cough which may include bloody sputum (called **hemoptysis**, himop' tisis), loss of appetite, weight loss, weakness, chills, night sweats, and fatigue. Because of the failure to eat and lack of sleep, a patient with untreated tuberculosis disease begins to waste away—which is why the disease was called "consumption." Lung hemorrhages can ultimately lead to death, as they did in the case of Vivian Leigh, the actress who played Scarlet O'Hara in the classic Hollywood movie *Gone with the Wind*.

Eighty-five percent of people who have tuberculosis have disease of the lungs; however, the bacilli can also cause disease of the lymphatic system, the genitourinary tract, and the covering of the brain, bones, and joints. How the disease progresses is dependent upon many factors including the age of the patient, the presence of coexisting diseases (HIV, diabetes, cancer, kidney disease, for example), and a history of the BCG vaccination against tuberculosis.

It actually is very difficult for the tubercle bacilli to establish infection and cause disease in a healthy human host. Repeated or prolonged exposure to another person with tuberculosis disease is usually necessary to spread the disease (which may be what happened on the long flight mentioned in the opening paragraph). Individuals who are homeless, living in poverty, are intravenous drug users, or HIV positive are most susceptible to infection. Poor general health, poor nutrition, other diseases, and overcrowding also contribute to increased host susceptibility and ultimately the development of tuberculosis disease.

The best way to prevent transmission of tuberculosis is to quickly identify infected individuals and provide treatment. Once identified, patients with tuberculosis disease may be hospitalized for treatment. Hospitalized patients should be in private rooms with special air handling and ventilation systems. If infected individuals must be treated at home, patients should be very careful around young children or other relatives and acquaintances who fall into the "susceptible" groups previously mentioned. The patient should be taught the proper way to cough safely and should sneeze only into disposable handkerchiefs which can then be appropriately destroyed.

# 5

# Transmission from Organism to Organism

The funeral home director/mortician was shocked when he was diagnosed with tuberculosis. He was not in any high risk group, had not traveled to a country where the incidence of tuberculosis is high, and had no friends, family, or co-workers with the disease. Where could he have possibly contracted his illness? Could it have been from one of the cadavers he had embalmed? To the mortician's surprise, when the DNA from his tubercle bacilli was compared to the strain of *Mycobacterium tuberculosis* that had killed one of the cadavers he had prepared, the strains were identical. It seems the bacteria had become airborne during the embalming process as the fluids which replaced blood moved through the cadaver's mouth and nose. This infusion probably created infectious aerosols which were inhaled by the mortician, resulting in disease.

## A GOOD SNEEZE AND A DEEP COUGH

A good sneeze expels over ten million germs; a deep cough expels a similar number. Yet germs or microbes are not released from these actions unprotected. Sneezes and coughs release organisms in drops composed of mucus (Figure 5.1). Many of the large drops fall to the floor or are inhaled or ingested where they are rendered harmless by being trapped in nose hairs or swallowed in saliva.

Some of the droplets dry and shrink. These droplets are light weight and easily carried on tiny air currents far and wide. *Mycobacterium tuberculosis* can float alive for hours or days protected from dehydration and harmful ultraviolet rays by the waxy coating surrounding the organism's cell wall.

**Figure 5.1** A sneeze, shown in this stop-action photograph, releases millions of mucous droplets. Bacterial and viral particles from respiratory diseases can be contained in this mucous and travel through the air. Unsuspecting people can inhale these droplets and get sick. This is why it is so important to cover your mouth and nose when you sneeze.

Dust particles also may trap expelled *Mycobacterium tuberculosis*. When the dust is resuspended by sweeping or by being kicked up, it may pose an infectious threat.

Tuberculosis infection as a result of ingestion of the organism is possible, but is about 10,000 times less effective than infection by inhalation. If the organisms are ingested they are often killed by the highly acidic conditions found in the stomach.

## SPECIAL RISKS TO HEALTH-CARE WORKERS

Health-care workers are at special risk from being infected with the tubercle bacilli. They are often exposed to undiagnosed tuberculosis patients, and those that work in prisons or shelters may be working under conditions of poor ventilation. Many of the activities that take place in a health-care setting such as suction and intubation are likely to produce respiratory aerosols which may contain tubercle bacilli.

In one hospital, during a 45 minute **bronchoscopy**, 13 people assisted with the procedure. Unfortunately, the patient was later found to have tuberculosis. Of the 13 people in the room, ten became infected by the tubercle bacilli.

Health-care facilities are now looking to protect their workers by installing special equipment. This equipment includes fans that will exchange the air in a patient's room between six and 12 times an hour and "negative pressure" rooms. Negative pressure prevents air currents from moving from the room into the hallway whenever the door to the room is opened. Rooms should be vented to the outside of the building and the venting tunnels equipped with ultraviolet lights to destroy bacteria that may get into the tunnel. Caregivers may wear respirators, although recently the use of respirators has become a subject of controversy—not everyone agrees the cost justifies the level of protection gained.

## DID YOU KNOW?

From the 1930s to 1960s, research aircraft sampled the air above earth and found large amounts of seeds and bacteria. A Russian rocket sampled the atmosphere 40 miles above earth and found bacteria. Clearly, organisms can travel very far on air currents.

## TUBERCULOSIS THREATS TO
## HUMANS FROM OTHER ANIMALS

Transmission of tubercle bacilli from animals to humans was first recognized in the early 1900s. In the United States, compulsory pasteurization (mild heat treatment of a liquid resulting in the destruction of disease-causing organisms contained within that liquid) was first adopted by Chicago in 1910 and then New York City in 1913. As a result, the public saw a major decrease in the number of children and young adults who developed tuberculosis from consumption of milk contaminated with *Mycobacterium bovis.*

Tuberculosis caused by *Mycobacterium bovis* is clinically identical to that caused by *Mycobacterium tuberculosis.* In countries where animal tuberculosis, particularly cattle tuberculosis, is not controlled, cases of tuberculosis still occur when humans drink or handle contaminated milk. In situations where the organism is ingested, scrofula, intestinal tuberculosis, and other non-pulmonary forms of tuberculosis are often seen.

No attempts are usually made to determine which species of acid-fast bacilli, either *Mycobacterium tuberculosis* or *Mycobacterium bovis,* has been isolated from the patient's sputum sample. Because *Mycobacterium bovis* is a rare cause of tuberculosis, it requires increased time and expense to correctly identify. Since drug treatment is the same regardless of which species of mycobacteria is causing the disease, public health clinics do not differentiate causes of tuberculosis. Therefore, the number of cases of tuberculosis being transmitted by animals to humans and caused by *Mycobacterium bovis* may currently be underestimated.

In many African countries cattle are an important part of human social life. Cattle in these countries represent wealth, and as such they are at the center of many social events and gatherings. On the continent of Africa, 85 percent of the cattle and 82 percent of the human population live in areas

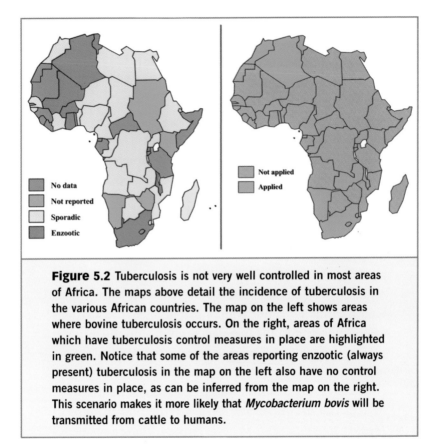

**Figure 5.2** Tuberculosis is not very well controlled in most areas of Africa. The maps above detail the incidence of tuberculosis in the various African countries. The map on the left shows areas where bovine tuberculosis occurs. On the right, areas of Africa which have tuberculosis control measures in place are highlighted in green. Notice that some of the areas reporting enzootic (always present) tuberculosis in the map on the left also have no control measures in place, as can be inferred from the map on the right. This scenario makes it more likely that *Mycobacterium bovis* will be transmitted from cattle to humans.

where bovine tuberculosis is only partially controlled or not controlled at all (Figure 5.2). In addition, pasteurization of milk is rarely practiced in these areas. The lack of tuberculosis control in cattle combined with the regular human exposure to cattle and the high rate of HIV infection in many parts of Africa make tuberculosis transmission from cattle to humans a serious public health concern.

In the United States, animal tuberculosis control and surveillance has been in effect since the early 1900s. In 1918, one of every 20 cattle tested positive for tuberculosis. In 1990, one of every 6,800 tested positive.

Since 1990, federal funds which support research and

surveillance of animal tuberculosis in the United States have been severely reduced. Cattle now spend a large amount of time in feedlots before moving onto very large, centrally located slaughterhouses. Many animals that arrive from all over the country and reside in one location for a period of time could give rise to a tuberculosis outbreak.

*Mycobacterium bovis* can cause tuberculosis in cattle, deer, elk, bison, and goats. Non-traditional animal production of deer, elk, and buffalo, or exotic animal farming of llama and alpacas raises the risk of an animal tuberculosis outbreak. An outbreak within animal herds carries with it the potential for human transmission.

## TUBERCULOSIS THREATS TO OTHER ANIMALS FROM HUMANS

In March 1996, five elephants from an exotic animal farm were in California as part of a circus act. One of the elephants died and upon examination after death, tuberculosis lesions were found in the lungs. Acid-fast bacilli were isolated from the first dead elephant. A second elephant died shortly afterwards. That elephant had visible respiratory and trunk exudates. Lung tissue showed caseous necrosis. Of the five elephants, three eventually died from tuberculosis and a fourth was found to be infected with *Mycobacterium tuberculosis*.

Elephant handlers worked closely with the elephants around the clock, and most lived in a building adjacent to the barn where the animals lived. All animal handlers, trainers, and caregivers were given tuberculosis tests, and 50 percent (11 of 22) of the handlers were positive with Mantoux testing (see Chapter 7 for an explanation of tuberculosis tests). Of the 11 with positive tests, one handler had an X-ray finding suggestive of active tuberculosis. The one handler with active tuberculosis and the infected elephant received multiple drug therapy. The remaining tuberculosis positive handlers received preventative drug therapy.

**Figure 5.3** Meerkats, pictured above, are social mammals that live in colonies of up to 30 animals. These small, insect-eating animals are native to the dry regions of Africa. As humans encroach upon their habitats, they are more likely to search for food around dwellings or in garbage dumps. Outbreaks among these wild animals are most likely the result of human contact and foraging for food. Tuberculosis can be especially lethal to these animals.

Elephants are not known hosts of the tubercle bacilli. Therefore, they must have been infected by one of their handlers. With three of the five elephants dying from tuberculosis, they are clearly a very susceptible animal group and infection is very lethal. The above scenario brings up an important consideration. How susceptible are animals to tuberculosis spread by humans, and how important is it to protect wildlife from this deadly disease?

With the AIDS epidemic affecting one-third of the population of Botswana, wildlife workers there are particularly concerned about protecting free-ranging wildlife. AIDS and tuberculosis are a common combination, and individuals who have AIDS may shed higher levels of the tubercle bacterium in their sputum. Two reports, an outbreak among banded mongooses and one among **meerkats** (Figure 5.3), emphasize the danger to wild animals from human tuberculosis. It is believed that both groups of animals contracted the disease by foraging in rubbish heaps outside human homes and a tourist lodge. Once the animals became infected, the disease moved quickly and lethally through their populations.

Ecotourism, travel to unique or pristine ecosystems to observe wildlife, has become very popular in many developing countries. This activity has increased the number of humans coming into contact with wild animals not previously exposed to tuberculosis. It remains to be seen how this increased contact will impact the incidence of airborne human diseases in wild animals.

# 6

# The Immune Response to Tuberculosis Infection

Tuberculosis fights a war with the body, and the lungs are often the battle field. On one side is the organism with its artillery and maneuvers, attempting to establish itself in the host for the long term. As with all parasites, the idea is not to kill the host, which would be self-defeating because the host provides the parasite with resources necessary for its survival, but only to dominate. On the opposing side is the host immune response. The first wave of troops includes the non-specific response ready to handle any invader. That initial defense is followed by the specific host immune response whose sole focus is to eliminate the specific organism causing the problem. The immune response seeks to take no prisoners. It is an all out war bent on eliminating the invader at all costs, even if some collateral damage ends up destroying host tissues.

## EARLY BATTLES
Once *Mycobacterium tuberculosis* reaches the lungs, patrolling lung macrophages ingest the bacteria (Figure 6.1). This ingestion occurs when the phagocytic cell engulfs the organism by sending out pseudopods (arm-like projections) to surround the bacterium. The ingested bacteria become enclosed inside the macrophage in a membrane-bound vacuole called the **phagosome.**

## THE HOST CELL ARSENAL
Within the phagocytic cell are **lysosomes** (lī' səsōms), which contain various lytic enzymes meant to destroy invading parties. When a lysosome

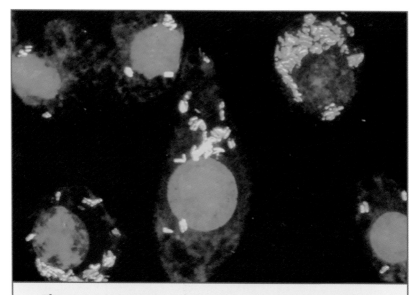

**Figure 6.1** Macrophages, an important part of the body's defense system, ingest foreign invaders in an attempt to prevent disease. In this picture, macrophages have ingested the tuberculosis bacilli. The macrophages are stained fluorescent green (the nucleus of each macrophage glows brighter than the rest of the cell), and the bacteria are stained fluorescent orange. Techniques such as fluorescent staining are often used to help scientists visualize cellular processes in the body.

fuses with a phagosome, a **phagolysosome** forms, and the contents of the lysosome are free to destroy the engulfed bacteria.

Inside the macrophage, a respiratory burst may occur resulting in the release of oxygen containing molecules (such as hydrogen peroxide) which also have the potential to destroy the bacteria. The macrophage can release various proteins and peptides which kill organisms, polyamines which combine with other compounds to form deadly hydrogen peroxide or ammonia, or iron chelators which make iron unavailable to the bacteria. Iron plays a key role in the process of bacterial respiration. Without iron, the bacteria cannot produce enough ATP (the fuel of the cell), and as a result, death occurs.

## THE BACTERIUM FIGHTS BACK

For every attack of the immune system, there is a counter attack by the organism. The tubercle bacilli can prevent fusion of the lysosome and phagosome, although the exact mechanism by which this occurs is unknown. This action is receiving a lot of attention as a possible antimicrobial target. Hopefully, genetic studies of *Mycobacterium tuberculosis* will provide more insight as to how to attack this specific point during infection.

If fusion does take place, some organisms may be able to escape the phagolysosome itself. *Mycobacterium tuberculosis* can release molecules which render toxic forms of oxygen harmless. These enzymes, **superoxide dismutase** and **catalase**, are normally used by the organism in any oxygen-containing environment. The organism can release substances which stimulate the macrophage to deactivate itself, making it ineffective in battle. Physical components of the bacterium, such as cord factor, may also be toxic to macrophages.

Very virulent tuberculosis bacteria cause the macrophage to burst, releasing organisms into the surrounding tissues. The released bacteria may be taken up by immature macrophages, too naïve or weak to kill the ingested organisms.

Waves of macrophages bursting, release of tuberculosis bacteria, and ingestion by weak macrophages give rise to the tubercle lesion (Figure 6.2), known generically as a **granuloma** (gran' yŏŏ lō mð), which begins to enlarge. Other immune cells

## DID YOU KNOW?

What is a cytokine or a lymphokine?

Both **cytokines** and **lymphokines** are regulatory molecules that cells produce to communicate with each other. They often function to increase the intensity of the specific immune response. Cytokines are produced by macrophages, natural killer cells, mast cells, and others. Lymphokines are special cytokines produced only by lymphocytes.

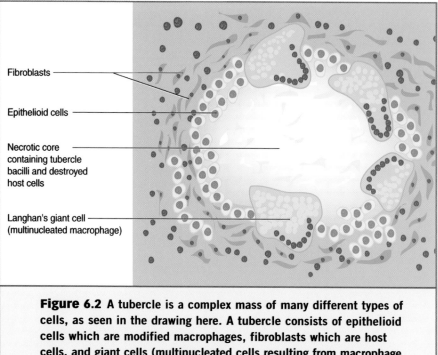

Fibroblasts

Epithelioid cells

Necrotic core
containing tubercle
bacilli and destroyed
host cells

Langhan's giant cell
(multinucleated macrophage)

**Figure 6.2** A tubercle is a complex mass of many different types of cells, as seen in the drawing here. A tubercle consists of epithelioid cells which are modified macrophages, fibroblasts which are host cells, and giant cells (multinucleated cells resulting from macrophage fusion). At the center of the tubercle are bacteria and the caseous necrosis that results from enzymatic destruction of host cells.

such as **monocytes** are recruited to the area by cytokines. These monocytes can transform into epithelial cells that also contribute to formation of the tubercle. The tubercle encapsulates, or walls off, the bacteria effectively reducing the available oxygen for the organisms. Organisms will begin to reproduce slowly, if at all, in the lesion.

### THE COUNTER ATTACK

In the meantime, the specific immune response is marshaled and T lymphocytes, also called **T cells**, begin to arrive. Macrophages that have been successful at killing bacteria activate T cells. These activated T cells secrete **lymphokines** which impact other cells and tissues in many ways (Table 6.1).

**Table 6.1** Important cytokines, their sources, and functions involved in the host response to tuberculosis infection.

| CYTOKINE NAME | SOURCE | ACTION |
|---|---|---|
| **Interferon** gamma | T lymphocyte and natural killer cells | Activates macrophages |
| Interleukin 1 | Macrophage, epithelial cells | Proliferation of T lymphocytes, promotes macrophage production of cytokines |
| Interleukin 6 | T lymphocytes Macrophage | Promotes T and B lymphocyte growth |
| Interleukin 10 | Macrophage, Mast cells | Decreases rate of reproduction of T lymphocytes, promotes antibody production |
| Interleukin 12 | Macrophage | Activates natural killer cells, influences T cells to release other cytokines |
| Tumor Necrosis Factor | T lymphocyte | Activates primed macrophage and natural killer cells, stimulates cytotoxic T lymphocytes. |

Some of the activated T cells may be cytotoxic, or killers of other cells. Cytotoxic T cells attack and destroy host macrophages that have ingested tuberculosis bacilli. Uninfected host cells may be accidentally destroyed by the large concentration of cytokines released at this point. Experienced macrophages release factors which promote formation of blood clots in blood vessels. These clots result in a lack of oxygen to the tissues resulting in tissue death.

If the actions of T cells and macrophages can control the progression of the lesions and the spread of bacilli, the disease will be arrested. The key battle strategy of the specific immune response is to destroy organisms wherever they may be before their numbers get too high. As a consequence, more tissue damage and cell destruction may be prevented.

## THE BATTLE LOST

If the immune response is unsuccessful and the bacterial concentration gets too high, then **liquefaction** of the tubercle will result. During liquefaction, the tubercle degrades because host cells which make up the structure are destroyed by the massive release of cell-destroying enzymes from other host cells. Once the lesion becomes liquefied, bacteria are no longer contained in phagocytic cells and begin to multiply uncontrollably. The bacteria multiply robustly because the concentration of oxygen is greater outside the phagocytic cell than inside. If the liquid spills into a nearby bronchiole, a cavity results. This cavity can be seen in an X-ray and provides clues when diagnosing tuberculosis disease. In the meantime, bacilli that have gained free access to the bronchii may be released during a cough only to infect other victims.

## A STALEMATE

If the number of bacteria remains low enough to be contained by the tubercle, the host immune response will subside, and the combatants reach a stalemate. The bacteria remain sequestered inside the lesion. This situation (latent tuberculosis) may last throughout the life of the victim. If something should happen to change the immune status of the host, such as HIV infection, an organ transplant, or steroid therapy for arthritis, this latent or arrested disease may reactivate.

Approximately 60 million people around the world have active tuberculosis, so it would seem that the immune system is outmatched against the tuberculosis bacterium. Yet given that an estimated 1.7 billion people worldwide may have been infected without developing the active disease, the host immune response must be winning more wars than the organism.

# 7

# Screening for and Diagnosis of Tuberculosis

In his search for a cure for tuberculosis, Dr. Koch observed that animals infected with tuberculosis developed a lesion at the site of inoculation if a substance called tuberculin was injected. Tuberculin, or old tuberculin as it is now known, was prepared from filtered, heat-sterilized cultures of *Mycobacterium tuberculosis*. Before use, the filtrate was evaporated to ten percent of its original volume. While this concentrate proved to be of no value in preventing tuberculosis (Chapter 2), several scientists of the time felt the reaction observed could be of some value as a screening tool for exposure to the organism.

## THE SEARCH FOR A SPECIFIC, REPRODUCIBLE SCREENING TOOL

One of those scientists, Austrian physician Clemens von Pirquet, first used the term *allergy* (from the Greek *allos ergos,* meaning altered energy) to describe a positive reaction to old tuberculin. He used the word *anergy* (Greek for without energy) to describe the lack of reaction to old tuberculin. The term anergy is often found today in information describing the lack of response to tuberculin testing by HIV positive individuals.

As researchers searched for the best way to use tuberculin as a screening tool in the early 1900s, one French physician, **Charles Mantoux,** introduced the technique of inoculating tuberculin just below the skin. This method of screening, developed in 1908 and known as the Mantoux test, is the preferred method of screening in use today. Although the Mantoux technique of screening was widely accepted, there were still some problems with preparation of old tuberculin which at times proved unreliable due to its heterogeneous nature and non-specificity.

## MODIFYING OLD TUBERCULIN
## MAKES ITS USE MORE RELIABLE

In 1934, **Florence Seibert**, who worked at the Phipps Institute in Philadelphia, developed a technique to extract proteins from *Mycobacterium tuberculosis* after it was grown on culture media and killed by heating to 121°C at 15 pounds of air pressure. Her preparation, which came to be known as **purified protein derivative (PPD)**, allowed standardization of the product used for testing and provided specific and reproducible results. Other than the addition of a detergent to prolong shelf life, Dr. Seibert's formulation of PPD is used today to screen for tuberculosis.

## WHAT IS THE TEST DETECTING?

When tuberculin is injected into someone who has been exposed to *Mycobacterium tuberculosis*, a reaction will occur at the injection site. This reaction, which remains local, occurs because phagocytic cells and sensitized T lymphocytes (sensitive because of previous exposure to the organism) migrate to the area. Once at the site of inoculation, the cells which have migrated release chemicals which create an inflammatory reaction. Local activity of the phagocytic cells and other inflammatory cells causes a lack of oxygen and acidic conditions in the area which can lead to host tissue destruction. All of these activities take place in a 24–72-hour period. For that reason this response is called a **delayed** (does not occur quickly) **hypersensitivity reaction.**

In order to interpret the results, the reaction at the inoculation site is observed and measured. The resulting measurements are interpreted in conjunction with other identified risk factors.

### HOW IS THE TEST DONE?

Tuberculin may be delivered in one of two ways: either by a multiple puncture device (a **tine test**) or by injecting a specific amount under the skin (the Mantoux test).

The multiple puncture device has multiple tines (4–6) which introduce tuberculin in a pattern into the skin. These devices usually consist of a plastic handle attached to a stainless steel disc. Projecting from the disc are metal prongs about two mm in length (Figure 7.1). One type of multiple puncture device includes a spring-loaded gun with sterile cartridges

## DID YOU KNOW?

### What is Inflammation?

**Inflammation** is the body's response to tissue injury or invasion by a foreign substance. In the process of inflammation, damaged or invaded host tissue releases chemical signals that attract phagocytic cells and other immune cells to the area. These phagocytic cells ingest the invader, while the other immune cells release chemicals called cytokines to recruit more immune cells. Resulting from all this activity are the four classical indications of inflammation: redness, heat, swelling, and pain. Inflammation should be considered a good thing because it is the body's attempt to eliminate the invader and repair the damage. Sometimes, however, it can be an overzealous response and result in host tissue damage as in the case of hypersensitivity or allergic reactions.

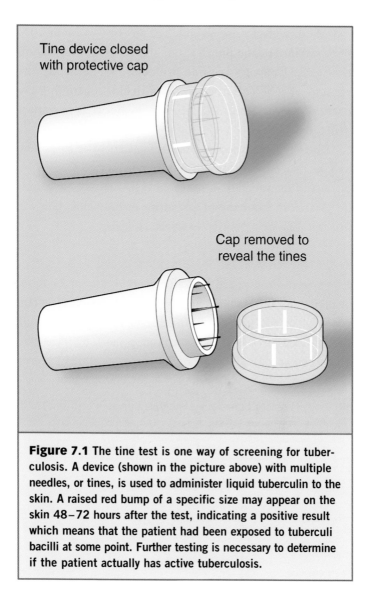

Tine device closed
with protective cap

Cap removed to
reveal the tines

**Figure 7.1** The tine test is one way of screening for tuberculosis. A device (shown in the picture above) with multiple
needles, or tines, is used to administer liquid tuberculin to the
skin. A raised red bump of a specific size may appear on the
skin 48–72 hours after the test, indicating a positive result
which means that the patient had been exposed to tuberculi
bacilli at some point. Further testing is necessary to determine
if the patient actually has active tuberculosis.

which deliver liquid tuberculin. When multiple puncture devices
are used, they must be in contact with the skin for at least one
second. The reaction produced should be measured within
48–72 hours. The patient may be given a card showing possible
reaction outcomes in order to make test interpretation easier.

Advantages of using the tine test are: ease of administration, stability of the preparation, and short administration time. Disadvantages include problems standardizing the amount of tuberculin delivered, difficulty controlling the depth of the puncture, and the time the device is in contact with the skin.

There is some discussion and disagreement as far as how well the tine test compares to the Mantoux method (Table 7.1). Because of the variation of results in large screening programs, the American Academy of Pediatrics recommends that the tine test no longer be used to screen children.

## THE MANTOUX TEST

It is now recommended that all screening for tuberculosis be done using the Mantoux method. In this technique, five **TU**s (tuberculin units, 0.1µg of PPD delivered in 0.1 ml of liquid) are delivered just under the skin using a short, blunt needle. The injection is usually made on the underside of the forearm

**Table 7.1** Differences between the multiple puncture test (tine) and the Mantoux tests for screening against tuberculosis infection.

|  | TINE TEST | MANTOUX TEST |
|---|---|---|
| Ease of administration | +++ | + |
| Time involved: preparation and administration | Less than 10 seconds | 1–2 minutes |
| Technical skill required to administer | N/A | Moderate |
| Most effective use | Large scale screening | Diagnosis of exposure to *Mycobacterium tuberculosis* |
| Ability to control antigen amount administered | Not good | Good |
| Stability of preparation and equipment | Stable | Must be protected from light and heat |
| Cost per use | $1.00 | $0.35 |

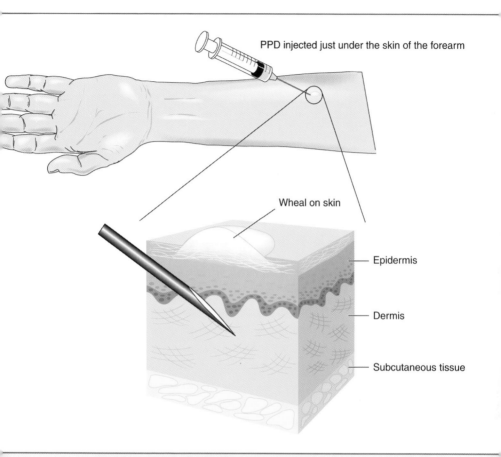

PPD injected just under the skin of the forearm

Wheal on skin

Epidermis

Dermis

Subcutaneous tissue

**Figure 7.2** The Mantoux test is another method used to test for tuberculosis. A short, blunt needle is used to deliver Purified Protein Derivative (PPD) just under the skin, and a small wheal, or bubble, should appear on the surface of the skin. The area where the test is administered is evaluated in 48–72 hours. Similar to the tine test, a hard raised bump indicates a positive test.

by placing the needle, flat side up, into the skin at a shallow angle (Figure 7.2). As the fluid is delivered, it should produce a **wheal** (wēl), a pale fluid-filled bubble six to ten millimeters (mm) in size just under the skin. This bubble will eventually disappear and the area should be evaluated in 48–72 hours.

## INTERPRETATION OF THE REACTION

Test results should be interpreted between 48 and 72 hours after the test is performed. When interpreting the results, only the hard raised area, called the **induration**, should be measured. Any redness surrounding the induration should not be included in the measurement. (Figure 7.3) Although Mantoux described a positive test as being the size of a two franc coin, we now know that the measurements mean different things for different at-risk groups.

For an individual who has no known risk factors for contracting tuberculosis, an induration measuring 15 millimeters or more indicates exposure to *Mycobacterium tuberculosis*. It does not mean the individual has tuberculosis disease. Additional tests and observations should be made before reaching that conclusion.

An induration zone of ten mm or more should be considered positive for individuals who fall into the following high risk groups:

- IV drug users

- Non-United States born persons from high-risk areas such as Asia, Africa, and Latin America

- An individual who has suffered a weight loss greater than ten percent of body weight

- Children exposed to adults at high risk

- Individuals with medical risk factors including diabetes, cancer, and kidney disease

- Residents of long-term care facilities (prisons, nursing homes, psychiatric facilities)

- Health-care workers and employees who provide services to any of the above mentioned groups.

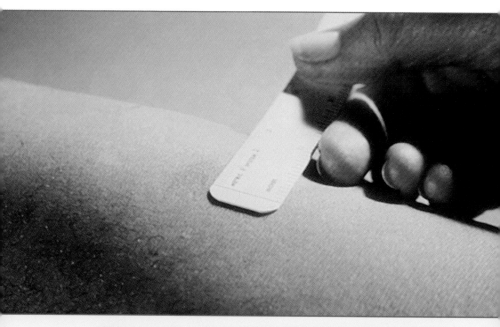

**Figure 7.3** After delivery of either the tine or the Mantoux test, the injection site must be evaluated for the presence of a bump. The bump is usually measured with a ruler, and the size of the reaction will indicate a positive test. However, the size necessary for a positive test differs depending on the type of test used and the patient's medical history.

An induration measuring five mm or more should be considered positive for individuals in the following groups:

- HIV positive individuals

- Individuals with chest X-rays consistent with healed tuberculosis lesions

- Individuals in recent contact with others who have active diagnosed tuberculosis

- Individuals undergoing therapy which suppresses their immune system such as organ transplant patients.

## BEYOND SCREENING

If an individual responds positively to the screening test, additional steps should be taken to confirm the diagnosis. The patient should be screened for other clinical signs and symptoms typically associated with tuberculosis. These include cough, fever, failure to gain weight, or weight loss. The health-care worker should keep in mind that forms of tuberculosis other than pulmonary tuberculosis may manifest themselves with different signs and symptoms.

Chest X-rays should be performed to look for changes in lung tissue and enlargement of lymph nodes in the area. Sputum cultures should be obtained to look for acid fast bacteria.

It is up to the physician to decide when to begin antibiotic treatment. For patients who belong to the high risk groups, the doctor may begin antibiotic therapy before the diagnosis is conclusive. In the case of some high risk individuals, much host damage could occur if the patient is not treated immediately.

## COMPLICATIONS AND DRAWBACKS OF TESTING

Adverse reactions to the screening tests are rare. However, upon repeated testing, non-responders (no initial reaction to Mantoux testing) may produce induration, a phenomenon

## DID YOU KNOW?

### Is it spit or sputum?

It is important when looking for acid-fast bacteria to have the right sample. If you are asked for a sputum sample, be sure you do not provide spit. What is the difference? Spit is saliva and material from the mouth, whereas sputum is material coughed up from the lung. In the case of tuberculosis, sputum will contain acid-fast bacteria, spit will not.

known as **boosting**. There may be some variability in response to tuberculin depending upon the immune status of the host. For example, AIDS patients rarely respond to screening although they may have active tuberculosis. These individuals are anergenic because they have a limited (if any) T cell population.

Anyone who has been vaccinated with BCG (Chapter 8) will usually react positively to the screening test. People infected with non-tuberculosis mycobacteria may also produce a positive reaction.

# 8

# The BCG Vaccine

More people in the world are vaccinated against this particular infectious disease than any other. Is it polio, tetanus, measles, chicken pox, or hepatitis? Actually, more humans are alive today that have been vaccinated against tuberculosis than any other disease, yet most people in the United States have not received the vaccine, let alone ever heard of it. Although administered for the past 80 years, this stable, safe, and relatively inexpensive vaccine remains controversial.

## HISTORY OF BCG

In the early 1900s, **Albert Calmette** and **Camille Guérin** were working at the Pasteur Institute in Lille, France. In 1906, Calmette observed that guinea pigs seemed to be protected from tuberculosis disease when they were first fed a horse strain (weakly infectious in humans) of the tubercle bacilli and then infected with a more virulent strain of the organism. Calmette and Guérin then began to study *Mycobacterium bovis*, a close relative of *Mycobacterium tuberculosis* that can also cause the disease in human beings. They had trouble with the organism clumping during growth, so they added ox bile to their potato-based growth media in hopes of changing the culture characteristics of the organism.

Calmette and Guérin were familiar with the techniques of Pasteur, the institute's namesake, who attenuated (weakened) the ability of viruses to cause disease by serial passage in a host. They sought to follow in the footsteps of Pasteur, so they transferred their strain of *Mycobacterium bovis* many times (231 times, over the course of 13 years) in media until the organism could no longer cause disease (as a byproduct, it also no longer clumped).

Calmette and Guérin spent the next several years infecting cattle, guinea pigs, monkeys, pigs, and chimps, and showed that their strain, **BCG** (**B**acille **C**almette **G**uérin), did not revert to one that could cause disease. In 1921, they received the opportunity to try the vaccine on humans. Calmette and Guérin administered their BCG strain to a newborn whose mother had died of tuberculosis. The child's grandmother, with whom she would live, also had the disease. The newborn received the vaccine on the third, fifth, and seventh days after birth. The vaccine proved to be a success! There were no harmful side effects, and from then on, the child remained free of tuberculosis for the rest of her life. Over the next six years, 969 children were vaccinated. Only 3.9 percent of them died from tuberculosis or other causes. Use of the vaccine gained public as well as governmental support, culminating in the recommendation of BCG for use against tuberculosis by the League of Nations in 1928.

Unfortunately, a major catastrophe involving use of the vaccine occurred in 1929 in Germany. Two hundred fifty-two children were vaccinated, of whom 72 died. Later it was discovered that a mistake was made at the lab which prepared the vaccine. Somehow, a disease-causing strain had contaminated the culture that was used to make vaccine. Although the mistake was found and the BCG vaccine vindicated, in the public opinion, damage was done. Albert Calmette (Figure 8.1) took this failure personally, and, it is said, as a result, he died a disheartened man in 1933.

**Figure 8.1** Albert Calmette, pictured here, worked with Camille Guérin
to develop a tuberculosis vaccine. They continually grew a strain of
tuberculosis until it was no longer infectious, and then used that strain
to infect animals. This led to their discovery of a human tuberculosis
vaccine, which is still used in several countries throughout the world,
although not in the United States.

## CURRENT VACCINE PRODUCTION

The World Health Organization currently oversees production and distribution of the tuberculosis vaccine. Three different strains of the organism are now used around the world to produce the vaccine. Although the three strains were derived from the original strain of Calmette and Guérin, the organisms have since been grown under different conditions and in different laboratories. These different cultural conditions have given rise to mutations in the strains resulting in differences in appearance, ability to grow and survive, rate of growth, and ability to induce an immune response in the host.

To produce the vaccine, the organism is grown on the surface of liquid media for six to nine days. The organism is then harvested and the resulting clump is broken up into a homogeneous suspension. The preparation is freeze-dried and resuspended in either saline or distilled water. To avoid further differences in strains and to attempt to maintain production equality, no original stock culture each laboratory possesses is to be transferred more than 12 times.

## SAFETY OF BCG

Limited side effects occur following vaccination. Some induration and ulceration at the vaccine site may be seen, and a vaccine scar may form as a result of inoculation. Severe neurological and other fatal complications resulting from vaccination are very rare and reported far less than for other available vaccines. It is important to note that HIV positive individuals should not receive the vaccine as they may actually develop disseminated tuberculosis infection due to the weakness of their immune systems. The United States remains one of the few industrialized nations not to use BCG on a national scale.

## HOW WELL DOES THE VACCINE PROTECT AGAINST TUBERCULOSIS?

Although safe and relatively inexpensive, the effectiveness of the vaccine remains a topic of considerable debate. Studies of vaccinated groups report effectiveness ranging from zero to 75 percent, with an average of 50 percent effectiveness in preventing tuberculosis. These differences in protective rates may be due to variation in vaccine production, vaccine administration, gender of the recipient, genetic differences of populations, age of the recipient, nutrition, socioeconomic status, history of previous exposure, stage of diagnosis, and follow-up after vaccination.

Although the exact percentage of effectiveness continues to be debated, most researchers agree that the vaccine works best in children, providing better than 80 percent protection against serious forms of the disease. The vaccine provides more protection against disseminated disease than pulmonary disease. Recent reports have suggested that the vaccine may provide some cross-protection against leprosy, a disease caused by *Mycobacterium leprae.*

### THE SEARCH FOR NEW VACCINES

Given the debate over BCG and the uneven immune response produced as a result of vaccination, effort is currently being placed on the development of new vaccines. With the sequencing of the *Mycobacterium tuberculosis* genome, it is hoped that genes associated with virulence can and will be identified (Chapter 3). Once identified these genes could be deleted, creating attenuated strains of bacteria, which could be used as a vaccine that would produce effective host immunity but not harm the host.

Genomics can also provide clues as to the nature of the antigens that induce a host immune response. These antigens could then be cloned in a non-infectious bacterium and used in a vaccine to produce immunity. A vaccine of this kind would be compatible with tuberculin testing that is currently done in the United States because it would not interfere with test outcome.

To combat pulmonary tuberculosis, new ways of delivering the vaccine are being investigated. Delivery of the vaccine via the respiratory route rather than through injection would theoretically provide better protection in the lungs and thus prevent pulmonary infection.

## DID YOU KNOW?

### The History of Vaccination: How Cowpox Helped Lead to the Elimination of Smallpox

The term vaccine is derived from *vacca,* the Latin word for cow. The practice of preventing disease by inoculation began with variolation, an ancient East Asian custom of exposing oneself to fluid from smallpox lesions to prevent development of a lethal smallpox infection. Centuries later, in 1716, Lady Mary Wortley Montegu, who was the wife of the British ambassador to Turkey, witnessed Turkish women inserting matter from smallpox lesions into the veins of villagers. Following a brief, mild illness the villagers recovered with no smallpox scars. Lady Montegu tried to convince the British Empire to adopt the practice, to no avail. Finally in 1798, the practice of vaccination became generally accepted thanks to Edward Jenner, an English country doctor. Dr. Jenner learned that milkmaids who contracted cowpox (the bovine form of smallpox and a common consequence of the milking profession) were not susceptible to smallpox. He utilized material from cowpox lesions of milkmaids to vaccinate his patients against smallpox. Smallpox remains the one and only infectious disease eradicated thanks to an effective vaccination program.

## BCG IS NOT RECOMMENDED
## FOR USE IN THE UNITED STATES

BCG is not recommended for use in the United States because the vaccine induces an immune response in the recipient which may cause a consequential response during Mantoux testing. Following BCG vaccination, interpretation of the screening test would be complicated because of the difficulty differentiating a reaction due to actual infection by the bacilli or one caused by the BCG vaccine. The benefits of BCG vaccination may also be outweighed by the fact that the risk for tuberculosis is relatively low in the United States compared to other parts of the world.

In lieu of vaccination, United States public health officials have developed a three point strategy to combat the disease. The strategy includes the following points: 1) early detection and treatment, 2) antibiotic therapy for people who are infected but do not have clinical disease, and 3) prevention of institutional (prisons, hospitals) transmission by employing effective tuberculosis control programs.

Although not recommended for routine use, there are some situations, in which the vaccine may be administered in the United States. Qualifying for vaccination includes people who fall into the following groups:

- Children who are continuously exposed to an untreated person with infectious pulmonary tuberculosis if the child cannot be removed from the home

- Children who are continuously exposed to someone with **multiple drug resistant tuberculosis** (MDR-TB) if they cannot be removed from the home

- Health care workers in a setting with a large number of MDR-TB individuals and where conventional tuberculosis control programs have not been successful

BCG is not recommended in the following instances:

- For adults or children with HIV, as well as other immunocompromised individuals

- As a requirement for employment of health care workers

- For pregnant women

- For health care workers in settings where the risk of transmission is low.

# 9

# Treatment of Tuberculosis I: Sanatoriums and Early Drug Treatments

In the last two decades, tuberculosis has reemerged, causing over two million deaths annually. The emergence of AIDS has contributed to the increased case rate of tuberculosis in industrialized countries. AIDS, civil wars, weakened economies, and the lack of public health programs have all increased the rates of tuberculosis in less-developed countries. What makes the incidence of this disease so shocking is that the increase in tuberculosis cases comes at a time when effective antimicrobial treatments are available to treat the disease and kill the organism. These effective treatments were not always available. In the past, cures, concoctions, and approaches to treating tuberculosis have been varied, and the results were often deadly.

## EARLY TREATMENTS

In ancient times, most disease was thought to be due to an imbalance of body humors (body fluids believed to be responsible for one's personality and health). To regain the balance, bloodletting was a classical treatment. From the era of Hippocrates through the twentieth century, bleeding of the patient was an accepted, if not particularly effective therapeutic approach to treating tuberculosis. The combination of bloodletting with the hemorrhaging that sometimes occurred in the lungs surely sent many patients to their deaths prematurely.

Since tuberculosis was considered a wasting disease, a common therapy was to provide a nutritional diet. Both Galen and Hippocrates recommended the consumption of milk and avoidance of meat and alcohol, both thought to cause a major imbalance of the humors. Hippocrates defined the diet even further by suggesting that the patient should avoid beef, but properly cooked pork was permitted and could promote healing. The diet recommendations of Galen and Hippocrates were followed through the 1800s. In addition, sweet elixirs for cough supplemented with opia camphorate (opium) were recommended.

As the science of chemistry developed in the 1800s, several chemical cures or treatments were used for tuberculosis. Chloride of sodium, chloride of lime, chlorine gas, digitalis, hydrocyanic acid, iodine, and creosote were among the compounds used to treat tuberculosis. The value of these remedies is debatable, and their use may have hastened the death of more than a few tuberculosis patients. However, it is interesting to note that a synthesized form of creosote,

## DID YOU KNOW?

Creosote is an oily liquid derived from either wood tar or coal tar. Creosote is often used to coat railroad ties or landscaping timbers to protect the wood from the elements. The active antimicrobial compound in creosote is cresol, a phenolic (containing phenol) compound. Phenols have both antibacterial and antiviral properties and are often used as disinfectants.

guafenesin, can still be found today in cough drops or cough syrups used to quiet a chronic cough.

Perhaps one of the most unusual attempts to cure tuberculosis took place in Mammoth Cave, Kentucky. In 1839, Mammoth Cave was purchased by a Louisville physician, Dr. John Croghan. Dr. Croghan was particularly interested in the healing properties of the caves. He believed the cave's constant temperature and humidity might help those suffering from tuberculosis.

Dr. Croghan admitted patients to wood and stone dwellings that had been constructed along the central trails in the cave in the spring of 1842. Legend has it that if one visited the caves at this time, he or she would be greeted by the sight of pale, emaciated individuals inside the huts and the sounds of constant coughing. Unfortunately, the cool temperatures and high humidity seemed to make the patients worse and several died (moist climate fosters transmission of the disease). The experiment ended in failure, and those who survived were taken out of the caves.

Dr. Croghan himself died of tuberculosis in 1849. Today, one can visit the caves and still see two stone huts which remain from the failed experiment.

## IN DR. CROGHAN'S OWN WORDS:

"At first they seemed much improved, though I now attribute this to their good spirits at the promise of a cure of their deadly malady. Later, however their conditions worsened, and before quite eight weeks had passed, several had given up the ghost while still inside the cave. The others I escorted back to the outer world, set them in carriages, and sent them home to await their fates."

National Park Service web site:
*http://www.nps.gov/maca/Explain7.htm.*

## THE SANATORIUM MOVEMENT

The industrial age brought with it large, crowded cities which were often smelly, filthy environments. Open sewers and poor attention to sanitation made the air unfavorable to the healing of a lung disease such as tuberculosis. Mild climates with clear mountain or salt air and pine forests were the direct opposite of city living and were often recommended as a cure. The search for treatment in a favorable climate gave rise to the construction of **sanatoriums** for the treatment of tuberculosis.

In 1854, Hermann Brehmer founded one of the first sanatoriums in the Bavarian Alps of Germany. The complex had 40 rooms, several common entertainment rooms, and a kitchen. The sanatorium was located in a mountain valley approximately 1,715 feet above sea level.

Brehmer believed that the small, weak hearts of tuberculosis patients (which he had seen as a medical student, studying the anatomy of cadavers) could be compensated for by living above sea level. This would allow the metabolism of the patients to improve and permit the body to heal itself of the offending disease, tuberculosis. Brehmer was encouraged in his assumptions by a German explorer who wrongly insisted that tuberculosis did not exist in populations who lived in mountainous regions.

Brehmer's sanatorium routine consisted of moderate exercise followed by rest, consumption of a nutritious diet, and the drinking of fresh spring water. By 1904, his sanatorium was the largest in the world and was able to accommodate 300 patients at a time. Dr. Brehmer's sanatorium, both in design and approach, soon came to be imitated all over Europe and in the United States.

The mountain resorts of Switzerland, particularly the village of Davos, were very popular with the wealthier victims of tuberculosis. This type of sanatorium, which featured elegant rooms, lavish meals, and minimal medical treatment, was the setting for the famous book by Thomas Mann, *The Magic*

**Figure 9.1** Edward Livingston Trudeau, pictured above, suffered from tuberculosis before moving to the Adriondack mountains in 1873. During his time there, his health improved, and he believed that the mountain air would do that same for others suffering from the disease. Dr. Trudeau opened a sanatorium on Saranac Lake, the first tuberculosis sanatorium in the United States. When he was not treating tuberculosis patients, he conducted experiments with the tubercle bacillus.

*Mountain.* In Mann's story the hero, Hans Castorp, spends seven years recovering from tuberculosis only to bid readers farewell as he runs through cannon fire in World War I.

The American sanatorium movement began with Edward Livingston Trudeau (Figure 9.1) who went to the Adirondacks in 1873, two years after his graduation from medical school, expecting to die from tuberculosis. He was very familiar with the

**Figure 9.2** The first building of Trudeau's sanatorium was a cottage called "Little Red." This building housed the tuberculosis patients who hoped that the clean mountain air would rid them of their tuberculosis. Little Red, pictured here, and Trudeau's sanatorium started a large sanatorium movement in the United States. Within 50 years, the United States had over 600 such facilities.

disease after having taken care of his brother who was diagnosed and died of tuberculosis in a short, four-month period. Trudeau expected the same fate. However, while in the Adirondacks his health improved. He moved back to New York City, became ill, and then improved again upon moving back to Saranac Lake (118 miles north of Albany, New York).

With financial help from his friends and other generous donors, Trudeau purchased some land in Saranac Lake and began construction of a cottage on the property. The cottage, Little Red (Figure 9.2), would provide housing for tuberculosis patients who would, hopefully, improve as Trudeau had.

In 1885, Trudeau admitted two patients to the cottages he had constructed. He also set up a laboratory on the grounds. After reading a translation of Koch's work on the infectious nature of tuberculosis, he managed to grow the tubercle bacillus, repeat Koch's experiments, and even test for the organism in samples from his patients' sputum. The Saranac Lake laboratory was the first in the United States to study tuberculosis. From its simple beginnings, the Trudeau Institute at Saranac Lake went on to train ex-patients to be nurses and provide post-graduate education at the Trudeau School for Tuberculosis, established in 1916.

Trudeau died of his tuberculosis in 1916 (age 68). Although he did not see many cures, he did start a movement. By 1904, there were 115 sanatoriums in the United States, by 1923, 656 facilities, and by 1953, 839 facilities that could care for 130,322 tuberculosis patients (Figure 9.3).

Sanatoriums also had a hand in changing personal habits and fashions. Men were encouraged to shave their beards and trim mustaches so as not to trap sputum from their coughs. Consumptive women were advised to shorten their hair, wear lighter dresses, and raise their hems above ankle level to avoid gathering dust which might be contaminated with tubercle bacilli.

Some patients liked the sheltered, structured environment of the sanatorium; others considered it confining and isolating. The system did enable physicians to observe the disease in a controlled environment, and the isolation of patients in sanatoriums may have helped prevent transmission.

The incidence of tuberculosis declined during the period of sanatorium treatment, although this was probably due to many factors. Much medical advancement also occurred during this period. *Mycobacterium tuberculosis* was discovered as the causative agent, X-rays were discovered, and tuberculin, originally described by Koch as a tuberculosis cure, provided a means to diagnose infection with the organism.

**Figure 9.3** Following the opening of Dr. Trudeau's Saranac Lake sanatorium, many other such treatment centers quickly sprang up all over the country. Patients were encouraged to sleep outdoors, even in the cold weather, where fresh air would, hopefully, lead to their cure.

## THE ANTIBIOTIC ERA

The antibiotic era of tuberculosis treatment began in 1946 with the discovery and use of streptomycin to treat tuberculosis (described in detail in Chapter 2). Prior to the use of antibiotics, approximately 50 percent of patients with lung disease died. With the use of antibiotics, the mortality rate dropped to less than ten percent.

Although streptomycin resulted in successful treatment for some patients, in others the antibiotic failed to produce improvement. Some patients had severe allergic reactions to the drug and in others antibiotic-resistant tubercle bacilli began to emerge.

To avoid the problem of antibiotic resistance, it was found to be advantageous to use two or more drugs in combination. This combination proved to be successful because it was more difficult for mutant organisms to arise spontaneously through genetic change to more than one drug.

## DID YOU KNOW?

George Orwell, born Eric Blair, a famous British author who wrote the books *Animal Farm* and *Nineteen Eighty-Four*, began his war with tuberculosis in 1938. While spending time in a sanatorium in 1947, he was able to secure a shipment of streptomycin from the United States. At first the antibiotic helped Orwell, but then side effects started to appear. In Orwell's own words, "a sort of discoloration appeared at the base of my fingers and toenails; then my face became red and the skin began to flake off and a rash appeared all over my body, especially down my back . . . meanwhile my nails had disintegrated and my hair began to fall out in patches. It was very unpleasant." Not able to tolerate streptomycin treatment, Orwell died of tuberculosis in 1948. He was 46 years old.

B. Crick, *George Orwell: A Life*, (London 1988) p.560.

The combination of para-aminosalicylic acid (PAS) and streptomycin worked better than streptomycin alone. Isoniazid and pyrazinamide were introduced in 1952 and proved almost 100 percent effective for tuberculosis patients. Both drugs had to be taken by the patient for almost a year and a half. This caused some problems with compliance because the drugs were expensive (it cost $3,500 to treat one patient with streptomycin and PAS) and on occasion produced side effects.

Rifampin was first made available in 1967. The combination of rifampin and isoniazid allowed the treatment time to be reduced from 18 to 6 months. Additional details regarding drug therapy can be found in the next chapter.

# 10

# Treatment of Tuberculosis II: Modern Drug Therapy

In the early 1990s, a man was infected with multiple drug-resistant tuberculosis (MDR-TB) in New York. Undiagnosed, he moved to South Carolina where he infected three family members and a neighbor. One of his family members later underwent a bronchoscopy, a procedure used to examine the airway branches that connect to the lungs. A bronchoscope is the name of the device inserted into the windpipe to view the area.

That same unsterilized bronchoscope was then used to examine six other people, five of whom eventually died from tuberculosis. The strain of tuberculosis which killed the five was designated the "W" strain. This strain arose in New York City in 1990 and is resistant to seven different drugs. Death rates from infection with the W strain can exceed 80 percent.

The above story illustrates the need to prevent development of MDR-TB as well as the need for quick diagnosis and appropriate treatment of active cases of tuberculosis.

## DRUG THERAPY

For the majority of patients, tuberculosis treatment includes an initial two-month course of therapy with four anti-tuberculosis drugs: isoniazid, rifampin, pyrazinamide, and ethambutol. This treatment is then followed by four months of isoniazid and rifampin only.

Ideally, the acid-fast bacillus should be isolated from the patient's

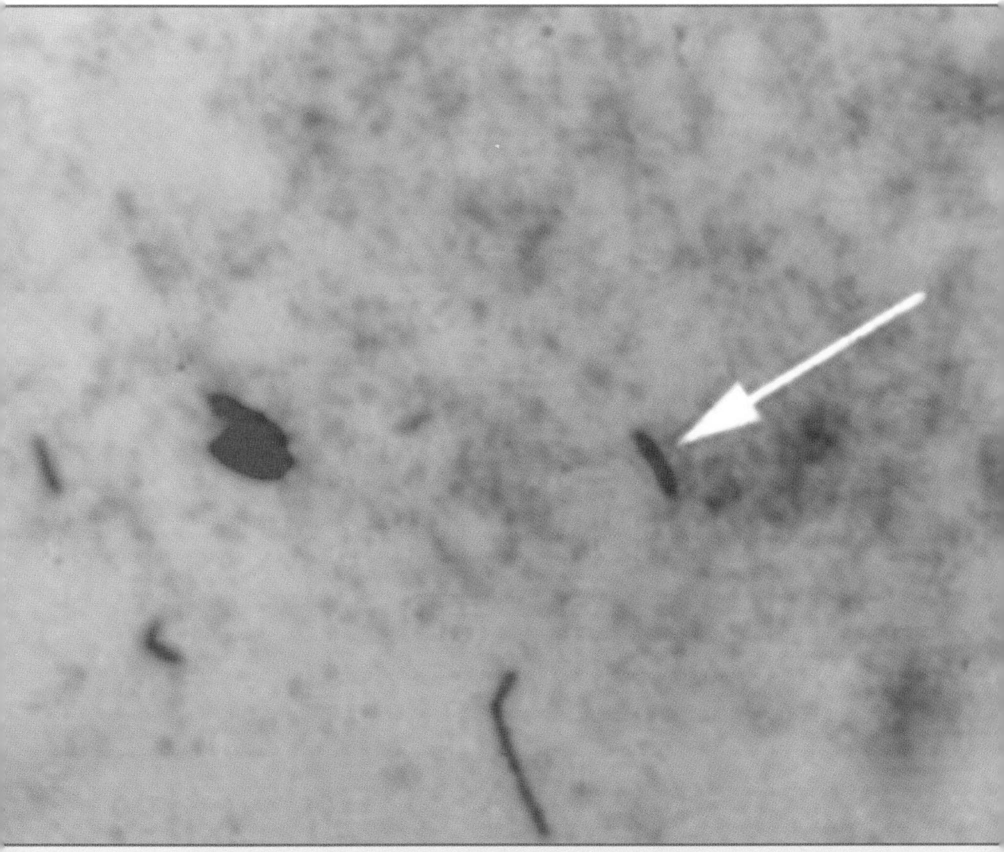

**Figure 10.1** Tuberculosis bacilli can be identified in a sputum sample using the acid-fast stain. Bacteria that are classified as acid-fast can retain a primary stain when washed with alcohol. These cells have a waxy cell wall which prevents alcohol from removing the initial stain. In the picture above, *Mycobacterium tuberculosis* cells, which are acid-fast, appear pink.

sputum (Figure 10.1). This isolate should then be tested for drug susceptibility to determine the most optimal course of antibiotic therapy. Unfortunately, because of slow bacterial growth, it takes at least three weeks to test for drug susceptibility.

Because time is of the essence, it is best to begin treatment with the four drugs before drug susceptibility is determined.

Treatment can then be modified based upon susceptibility tests. In the case where the chance of drug resistance of the isolate is low, three drugs may be adequate for treatment. However, at least two drugs must always be used to treat tuberculosis disease in order to prevent the emergence of drug resistant bacilli.

Some patients with tuberculosis infection, not disease, may be prescribed medication because of other risk factors. In this situation, a single drug, isoniazid, is prescribed for six to 12 months.

### WHY DOES DRUG RESISTANCE DEVELOP?

A bacterial strain is considered drug resistant if the frequency of drug resistant organisms in the bacterial population is one percent or greater. Initially, in drug-sensitive tuberculosis infections, one in 1 million bacilli is naturally resistant to isoniazid, and one in 100 million bacilli is resistant to rifampin. When treating a patient with one antibiotic, the drug resistant strain will continue to replicate and eventually outnumber the drug sensitive organisms. In a short time, a frequency of one percent drug resistant organisms can easily be obtained in the large bacterial populations found in active tuberculosis disease.

If two drugs are used to treat tuberculosis, the expected frequency of bacterial mutation to resistance to both drugs is

## DID YOU KNOW?

The tubercle bacilli become resistant to isoniazid in an unusual way. Instead of actively acquiring resistance, the organism loses its susceptibility to the drug. This happens when the bacilli loses the gene that encodes the enzyme that renders the bacterium vulnerable to the drug. This is possible because isoniazid has no antibacterial activity itself but requires the bacteria to produce an enzyme to convert the drug to an active antimicrobial form.

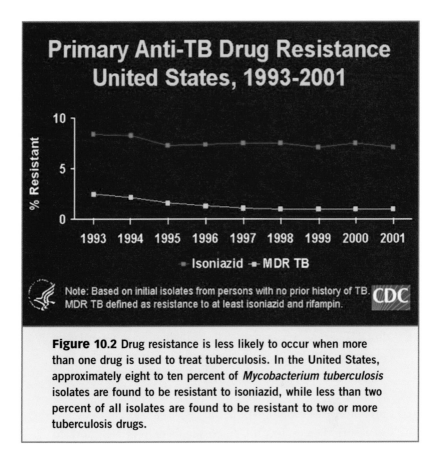

**Figure 10.2** Drug resistance is less likely to occur when more than one drug is used to treat tuberculosis. In the United States, approximately eight to ten percent of *Mycobacterium tuberculosis* isolates are found to be resistant to isoniazid, while less than two percent of all isolates are found to be resistant to two or more tuberculosis drugs.

one organism in a population of approximately $10^{14}$ to $10^{20}$. Because this frequency is so low, drug resistance is less likely to develop when more than two drugs are prescribed (Figure 10.2).

Multiple drug resistant tuberculosis (MDR-TB) is defined as resistance to two or more tuberculosis drugs. Drug resistance may emerge naturally at the rates described above. However, it is more likely to emerge as a treatment problem due to insufficient therapy, inappropriate therapy, and the failure of the patient to comply with prescribed therapy. Malabsorption of medications due to malnourishment may also contribute to the emergence of drug resistance.

## PREVENTING THE EMERGENCE
## OF MULTIPLE DRUG RESISTANCE

Treating someone with MDR-TB may cost up to $250,000 and take over two years. It is therefore imperative that initial treatment be continued for the appropriate period of time to prevent the emergence of drug resistant organisms. The patient must take all drugs as prescribed and not stop when they are feeling better. Patients often discontinue medication because of common side effects such as diarrhea and nausea. Unfortunately, stopping medication will give rise to multiple antibiotic resistant organisms.

## DIRECTLY OBSERVED THERAPY (DOT)

It is estimated that 20 percent of all tuberculosis patients fail to complete drug therapy. To insure that patients take their drugs as prescribed, **directly observed therapy** or DOT is employed. In DOT, a caregiver insures that the patient is taking drugs by observing their use directly (Figure 10.3). This approach is very expensive, and can tax public health resources. On the other hand, DOT is extremely effective at eliminating disease and preventing the evolution of MDR-TB.

DOT therapy was instituted successfully in New York to eliminate the tuberculosis that raged through Harlem in the early 1990s. Recently, an immigrant neighborhood in Queens called Corona utilized the same approach to quash a tuberculosis outbreak. In Corona, health care workers observe ten to 15 patients a day, five days a week, taking their medication. Patients who comply are rewarded with fast food coupons or food items.

Sometimes it is necessary to employ DOT under confined conditions. In New York City, the modern day version of the sanatorium has returned. Patients who fail to take their medication may be held against their will, confined to a tuberculosis ward in a hospital.

Goldwater Memorial Hospital in New York City is a

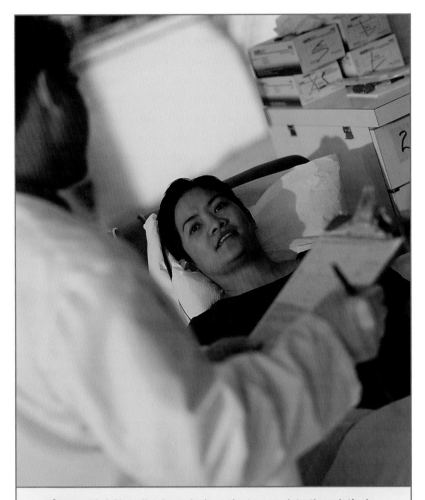

**Figure 10.3** Not all tuberculosis patients complete the relatively long process of drug therapy. However, without completing the recommended drug regimen, they are not cured of the disease and can pass it on to others. Directly Observed Therapy (DOT) is one way to ensure that patients take all of their prescribed medications. A DOT caregiver makes sure that the patient receives the proper medication by actually watching that person take the drugs. DOT is very expensive, but also very effective. In the picture above, a healthcare worker discusses methods of treatment with a patient. Patients who comply with the program often receive food coupons or monetary incentives.

facility where city health officials can detain tuberculosis patients for months until they are cured. Patients are not allowed out of the tuberculosis ward for the full term of treatment. They sleep in private or four-patient rooms complete with televisions and telephones. Other amenities include a recreation room with billiards, available drug treatment and psychiatric counseling, and educational tutoring.

Most patients complain that forced confinement to a tuberculosis treatment facility takes away their civil liberties. City health officials attempt to balance public health with private freedoms. Before a patient is confined, they are provided with a lawyer paid for by the city and have the right to fight in court against confinement.

Regardless of how it is applied, DOT cures disease, prevents transmission, and prevents the development of multiple drug resistance. Although proven successful, the World Health Organization reports that DOT has been slow to be fully implemented worldwide due in part to its cost and the requirement for a (government) public health infrastructure in the countries affected (Figure 10.4).

## TREATMENT OF DRUG RESISTANT TUBERCULOSIS

Patients who have drug-resistant tuberculosis may be required to take over 20 pills per day for a period of up to two years. The drugs employed will be "second line" drugs which are usually not as effective as the first choice drugs. These drugs usually cause more side effects and are more toxic to the host.

Second line drugs include ciprofloxacin, amikacin, ofloxacin, para-aminosalicylic acid, thionamide, and thiacetazone. Side effects from these drugs include kidney toxicity, neurotoxicity, severe gastrointestinal upset, skin problems, and liver toxicity. In addition to utilizing second line drugs to treat MDR-TB, surgery to remove infected tissue may be considered.

## 2. IMPLEMENTATION OF DOTS, 2000

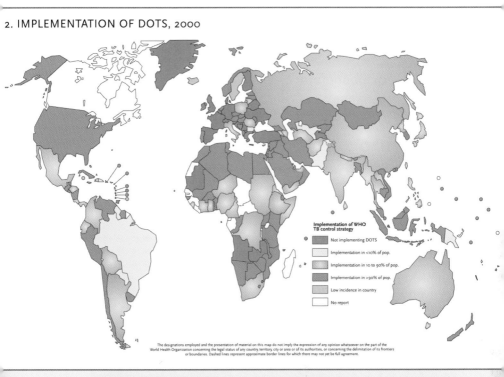

**Figure 10.4** Although DOT can be used successfully to cure tuberculosis and prevent disease transmission, implementation throughout the world has been slow to occur. The map above details the level of DOT implementation in various regions of the world. Many countries in the Americas and Africa have successfully implemented DOT, while countries in Europe, South-East Asia, and the Eastern Mediterranean regions have fewer DOT programs in place.

## THE SEARCH FOR NEW DRUGS

Because drug resistance continues to emerge, it is necessary to search for and develop new anti-mycobacterial medications. Sequencing of the tuberculosis genome has provided new information about the organism. Sequence information and the elucidation of gene function will provide information to develop new drugs (see Chapter 3). Of particular interest is the development of drugs which remain in the body longer. More stable drugs require fewer doses and shorter

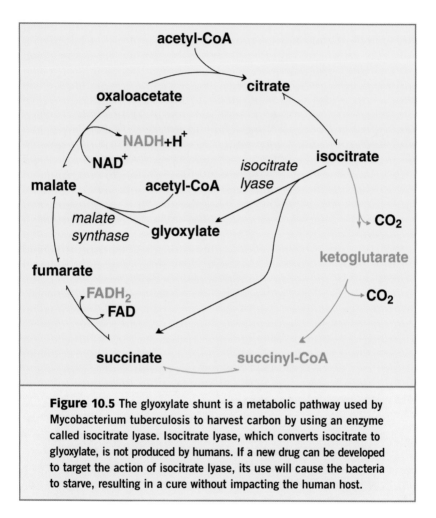

**Figure 10.5** The glyoxylate shunt is a metabolic pathway used by Mycobacterium tuberculosis to harvest carbon by using an enzyme called isocitrate lyase. Isocitrate lyase, which converts isocitrate to glyoxylate, is not produced by humans. If a new drug can be developed to target the action of isocitrate lyase, its use will cause the bacteria to starve, resulting in a cure without impacting the human host.

therapy. It is also important to develop drugs which do not interfere with anti-HIV medications since the HIV-positive population of individuals has greatly impacted the incidence of tuberculosis.

When treating tuberculosis with medication, it is important to remember that there may be two different populations of tubercle bacilli in the body: the rapidly growing organisms, which are easily and quickly killed by medication, and the more slowly replicating (or perhaps not growing at all) population of bacilli which require an extended course of drug therapy.

A group of researchers looking for new drug targets is focusing on the ability of the bacterium to exist inside the host cell for many years (latency). By studying the metabolism of the bacteria, scientists have learned that rather then yielding carbon from the breakdown of sugars in a biological pathway called the Krebs cycle, mycobacteria inside the tubercle obtain carbon from fats via a pathway called the glyoxylate shunt (Figure 10.5). To harvest the carbon, the organisms use an enzyme called isocitrate lyase. This enzyme is only produced in some animals, plants, and bacteria; it is not found in humans. Turning off this enzyme with a drug would starve the bacteria inside the tuberculosis lesion, resulting in a complete cure. Destruction of this molecular target would not cause side effects in the human host because the enzyme does not exist in host cells.

In addition to searching for new drug targets, pharmaceutical companies are also tinkering with currently used drugs to make them more effective. Rifabutin and rifapentine are derivatives of rifamycin which may be used instead of rifampin. Rifabutin appears to be more active against *Mycobacterium tuberculosis* than rifamycin (rifampin), without being more toxic to the host.

# 11

# The Human Immunodeficiency Virus and Tuberculosis

Five cases of a new life-threatening disease were first reported in Los Angeles in 1981. Patients appeared to have a bad case of influenza. Instead of recovering from their initial illness, the patients began dying from rare complications. These complications included a fungal lung infection caused by *Pneumocystis carinii* (new mō sistis kar ē nē) and a cancer of the blood vessels called Kaposi's (kap' əsēz) sarcoma. The rare complications of initial disease suggested that the patient's immune system was functioning poorly, if at all. The disease was given the name acquired immune deficiency syndrome, or **AIDS**, to reflect the fact that infected individuals had very impaired immune systems.

In 1983, French researchers at the Pasteur Institute provided evidence that AIDS was caused by a retrovirus. The virus, originally called lymphadenopathy virus (LAV), was designated human immunodeficiency virus, or **HIV**, in 1986.

AIDS patients have a sharp decrease in their population of T lymphocytes. These T lymphocytes are responsible for releasing lymphokines which recruit and activate macrophage and cytotoxic cells. As described in Chapter 6, lymphokines are very important in the specific immune response which prevents tuberculosis infection from ultimately developing into tuberculosis disease. HIV can also infect macrophages, other critical cells in the war against tuberculosis disease.

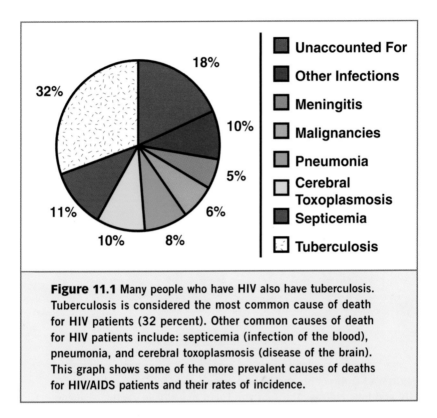

**Figure 11.1** Many people who have HIV also have tuberculosis. Tuberculosis is considered the most common cause of death for HIV patients (32 percent). Other common causes of death for HIV patients include: septicemia (infection of the blood), pneumonia, and cerebral toxoplasmosis (disease of the brain). This graph shows some of the more prevalent causes of deaths for HIV/AIDS patients and their rates of incidence.

## AIDS AND TUBERCULOSIS—DEADLY PARTNERS

The association between HIV and tuberculosis first became apparent in 1987 when diagnosis of disseminated tuberculosis became part of the case definition of AIDS. Tuberculosis is now considered the most common cause of death in persons with HIV infection (Figure 11.1).

In individuals who are HIV positive, the mortality rate from MDR-TB is between 70 and 90 percent with most patients succumbing to tuberculosis in an average of four months. To complicate matters further, 90 percent of all MDR-TB occurs in HIV positive individuals.

HIV infection promotes progression of tuberculosis infection to tuberculosis disease and tuberculosis disease may accelerate HIV replication. Persons with AIDS (see box

**2. Estimated incidence rates of HIV-positive TB, 1999**

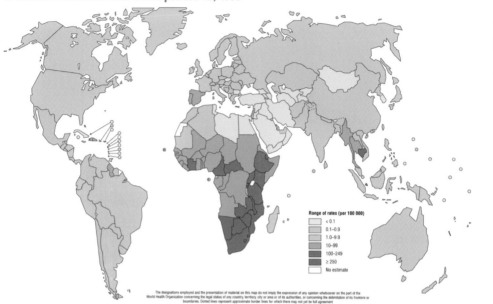

Range of rates (per 100 000)

| | |
|---|---|
| | < 0.1 |
| | 0.1–0.9 |
| | 1.0–9.9 |
| | 10–99 |
| | 100–249 |
| | ≥ 250 |
| | No estimate |

The designations employed and the presentation of material on this map do not imply the expression of any opinion whatsoever on the part of the World Health Organization concerning the legal status of any country, territory, city or area or of its authorities, or concerning the delimitation of its frontiers or boundaries. Dotted lines represent approximate border lines for which there may not yet be full agreement

**Figure 11.2** Africa has the highest reports of people infected with both HIV and tuberculosis. The southern tip of the African continent alone has over 250 patients per 100,000 people. The map pictured above, courtesy of the World Health Organization's Global Tuberculosis Control Report for 2002, details different incidence rates in each country throughout the world.

on page 93 for a discussion of HIV and AIDS) have rapidly progressing, newly acquired tuberculosis infection, and because of the detrimental effects of HIV on T lymphocytes, reactivation of latent tuberculosis is very likely.

The World Health Organization reports that nearly five million people worldwide are infected with both tuberculosis and HIV. Approximately three-fourths of them live in Africa (Figure 11.2). HIV has been blamed for a fourfold rise in the incidence of tuberculosis, particularly in the sub-Saharan region of the continent.

## DIAGNOSIS OF TUBERCULOSIS
## IN HIV POSITIVE INDIVIDUALS

In 1991, at a San Francisco residence for HIV positive individuals, 12 of 31 residents became infected with tuberculosis over a five-month period. Genetic evaluation of the infecting *Mycobacterium tuberculosis* strain showed that one resident had infected the rest. The preceding scenario demonstrates how quickly the tubercle bacilli can spread through a susceptible population.

Unfortunately, diagnosis of tuberculosis in HIV positive individuals may be difficult. Approximately 50 percent of those infected do not respond to the Mantoux test (anergy) because of weakened immune systems. In those individuals that do respond to testing, the size of the zone of induration may be smaller than expected, five mm or less. Length of HIV infection will determine the testing response as those individuals that are more recently diagnosed as HIV positive will produce a larger area of induration in the Mantoux test than those who have been

## WHAT IS THE DIFFERENCE BETWEEN SOMEONE WHO IS HIV POSITIVE AND SOMEONE WHO HAS AIDS?

An HIV positive individual, or someone who is infected with HIV, has had the virus enter the body and begin replicating. As HIV infection progresses, the virus continues to replicate and begins causing damage to the body, particularly the immune system. Strictly speaking, AIDS is the term used to describe the end stage of HIV infection. AIDS is characterized by immune deficiency, the development of tumors, and the occurrence of opportunistic infections. Almost everyone who is infected with HIV ultimately progresses to having AIDS and finally death.

diagnosed as HIV positive for an extended period of time. People who have been infected with HIV for many years are least likely to respond to a Mantoux test even though they may have active tuberculosis. Diagnosis of tuberculosis may further be complicated because of the difficulty encountered when attempting to culture tubercle bacilli from AIDS patients.

Because individuals with AIDS do not always respond to tuberculosis tests, there may be a delay in correctly diagnosing tuberculosis in these individuals. During this time, the patient can transmit tuberculosis unknowingly.

## CLINICAL FEATURES OF
## HIV POSITIVE INDIVIDUALS

The clinical features of tuberculosis infection will depend upon the health of the immune system of the HIV positive patient. Those infected with tuberculosis early during HIV progression have more typical tuberculosis disease with the upper portions of the lungs most often infected. As HIV infection progresses, tubercles usually develop more deeply in the lungs. Also in advanced HIV infection, or AIDS, tuberculosis will more likely be disseminated often resulting in inflammation of the membrane covering the heart (pericarditis), the lining of the abdomen (peritonitis), or the lining covering the brain and spinal cord (meningitis). The tubercle bacilli may also spread to bones and joints.

Expected X-ray findings such as spots related to calcified tubercles are seen in 50 percent or less of infected AIDS patients. Diagnosis is further complicated because pulmonary tuberculosis is easily confused with other opportunistic lung infections, Kaposi's sarcoma, or lymphoma.

## TREATMENT

Because the course of tuberculosis may be greatly accelerated in AIDS patients, treatment usually begins as soon as tuberculosis is suspected. HIV positive individuals often fail to respond to the Mantoux test; therefore, preventative therapy should be prescribed even when the tuberculosis test is negative. Preventative isoniazid is prescribed for 12 months to HIV positive individuals exposed to someone who has tuberculosis. For those in which tuberculosis has been diagnosed, the normal four-drug regimen is prescribed for a period of nine months (rather than six).

Patients with known tuberculosis and AIDS should begin treatment in an isolated environment for at least the first two weeks of therapy. Isolation should include housing in an individual room with a closed door and adequate ventilation. Air from the room should be exhausted to the outside of the building. Bactericidal ultra-violet light and air filtration should be used as a further precaution. Health-care workers coming in contact with the HIV/tuberculosis patient should periodically be tested for tuberculosis.

Directly observed therapy (DOT) is an absolute requirement for intravenous drug users and homeless individuals who have AIDS and tuberculosis. Special precautions regarding isolation must be taken in health-care settings when HIV positive individuals are treated. MDR-TB is especially prevalent in this environment.

AIDS patients often take five to ten medications to treat their disease. Anti-tuberculosis medication should not interact with the prescribed medications. Of particular concern is the interaction of protease inhibitors used to treat AIDS with rifampin. Protease inhibitors combined with rifampin have been shown to increase rifampin's toxicity. For IV drug users in treatment receiving methadone, special caution must be used because methadone can interact with rifampin.

The BCG vaccine should not be administered to HIV positive individuals in whom it can cause disease in the spine, cardiovascular system, or brain.

## ECONOMIC AND ETHICAL CONCERNS

In the New York Criminal Courts Building in Brooklyn, over 200 criminal suspects are herded into holding pens each day. Each 10 x 15 foot pen holds 12 or more detainees who stay two to three days. Many of the suspects are either homeless, are intravenous drug users, or have AIDS, while some individuals fall into all of the previously mentioned categories. Thousands pass through these unventilated holding pens each month. Corrections officers are afraid, lawyers are afraid, and even the inmates are afraid of catching a dreaded disease like tuberculosis in this environment.

Prisons, HIV, and tuberculosis are a deadly combination. Prisoners are housed in large groups, eating, living, and working together. Older prison buildings have poor ventilation. More than 80 percent of prisoners have used street drugs and approximately 65 percent of prison inmates have AIDS and tuberculosis. All of these conditions and factors combine to promote the transmission of tuberculosis in prisons.

Unfortunately, states have little money to provide appropriate isolation and treatment for infected inmates, although some states, New York in particular, have attempted to provide isolation wards to treat infected prisoners.

Homeless people that are HIV positive and have tuberculosis are of particular concern to public health workers. Once released from prison, these individuals need access to housing. Unfortunately, local governments are stressed trying to provide housing in a supervised environment before these inmates are released from prison or discharged from the hospital.

In states where HIV infection is common, only AIDS cases are reportable. There is no mandated treatment or confinement of the sexually active, HIV positive individual who may be infecting others. Tuberculosis control laws, on the other hand, include mandated testing, treatment and, if needed, confinement. These differences may be due to the fact that tuberculosis can be spread by casual contact (breathing) and also because the disease poses a serious health threat. This threat requires patient identification, isolation, treatment, and contact information. Knowledge of a patient's HIV status is essential to insure proper tuberculosis care. Balancing patient confidentiality regarding HIV and tuberculosis risk and infection will continue to be a challenge for public health care workers.

## WHAT'S NEXT?

It is clear that HIV/AIDS and tuberculosis is a global problem; so it will take a global effort to develop resources and strategies to eliminate both diseases.

In 1989, Public Health Service support in the United States for tuberculosis research totaled less than five million dollars. By 1999 that figure was approximately $70 million (National Institutes of Health and the Centers for Disease Control and Prevention). Now, with the introduction of the Comprehensive TB Elimination Act of 2001 (HR 1167), the United States House of Representatives has requested $528 million to fund tuberculosis programs managed by the Centers for Disease Control and Prevention. This allocation includes $240 million for the National Institutes of Health to award for basic tuberculosis research. The bill is currently being discussed in committee and sponsors are hopeful concerning its passage.

The annual cost of tuberculosis in the United States alone is estimated to be one billion dollars. Clearly, worldwide efforts aimed at treating and preventing the disease will be worth the cost. Regarding the HIV/tuberculosis partnership; "effectively treating tuberculosis will not solve the worldwide AIDS crisis but it will significantly reduce its burden."[2]

---

2. Dr. Peter Piot, Executive Director of the Joint United Nations Programme on HIV-AIDS (UNAIDS) in *Stop TB News*, Issue 4, Summer 2001.

# Glossary

**AIDS (Acquired Immune Deficiency Syndrome)** — The end stage of HIV infection characterized by opportunistic infections (infections caused by organisms that do not normally cause disease in a healthy human host). A patient with AIDS has a very low or nonexistent T lymphocyte count.

**Acid-fast stain** — A differential stain used to identify bacteria which have mycolic acids in their cell wall.

**Allergy** — An excessive immune response to a foreign substance.

**Anergy** — Lack of an immune response to a foreign substance.

**Antibiotic** — An antimicrobial substance produced by another living organism.

**BCG vaccine** — Bacille Calmette Guérin vaccine, originally formulated by Albert Calmette and Camille Guérin using *Mycobacterium bovis*. The vaccine protects against tuberculosis.

**Boosting** — An enhanced immune response to tuberculin testing due to repeated testing.

**Bronchoscopy** — A medical procedure in which a viewing instrument, a bronchoscope, is inserted into the trachea to view the upper area of the lungs.

**Calmette, Albert** — Founder of the Pasteur Institute at Lille, France. Along with Camille Guérin, he formulated the BCG vaccine.

**Caseous exudates** — Thick secretions resulting from the decay of the tubercle due to the release of enzymes by bacteria and host cells.

**Catalase** — An enzyme produced by many bacteria that detoxifies hydrogen peroxide by breaking it down into oxygen and water.

**Consumption** — Antiquated term for tuberculosis.

**Cords** — Filamentous aggregates of *Mycobacterium tuberculosis* observed when the organism grows in animal tissues.

**Cytokines** — Hormone-like proteins produced by cells of the immune response, particularly lymphocytes and macrophages.

**Delayed hypersensitivity reaction** — An exaggerated immune response involving T lymphocytes that manifests 48–72 hours after exposure to antigen.

**Directly observed therapy (DOT)** — An effective therapy which relies on health-care workers to directly observe administration of antitubercular medications to affected individuals.

**Droplet nuclei**—Small liquid droplets containing bacteria. Often released during sneezing or deep coughing.

**Galen**—Greek physican who was interested in studying tuberculosis and systems of the human body. His prescription for tuberculosis included rest, diet, and fresh/salt air and was followed for almost 1,700 years.

**Genome**—All of the genetic information contained in an organism.

**Giant cells**—Large, multinucleated cells which result from the fusion of macrophages. Giant cells are one component of a tubercle.

**Granuloma**—A lesion composed of macrophages, lymphocytes, bacteria, and host cells. The function of the granuloma is to wall off the infectious agent. In tuberculosis, a granuloma is called a tubercle.

**Guérin, Camille**—French veterinarian who, along with Albert Calmette, first produced the BCG vaccine.

**HIV (Human Immunodeficiency Virus)**—A virus which infects T lymphocytes. The infection ultimately results in a depressed or absent immune response.

**Hemoptysis**—Coughing up blood from the respiratory tract.

**Induration**—A hard raised area on the skin.

**Inflammation**—A host response to foreign substances or tissue damage. Inflammation is characterized by redness, heat, swelling, and pain in the area where it occurs.

**Interferon**—A cytokine produced by T lymphocytes. Interferon can activate macrophages.

**Koch, Robert**—German doctor and Nobel prize winner who observed and identified *Mycobacterium tuberculosis* as the cause of tuberculosis in 1881.

**Koch's postulates**—A series of steps put forth by Robert Koch that are designed to identify the particular organism which causes a specific disease.

**Latent tuberculosis**—A non-infectious form of tuberculosis in which the bacteria are sequestered inside tubercles.

**Liquefaction**—Process by which tissues become liquid due to of the release of enzymes from cells.

**Lymphocytes**—Cells which function in the specific immune response to eliminate foreign bodies or organisms. B lymphocytes produce antibody, whereas T lymphocytes release cytokines or kill other cells.

**Lymphokines**—Cytokines produced by lymphocytes.

**Lyse**—To break open.

**Lysosome**—A structure, particularly in macrophages, which contains digestive enzymes.

**Macrophage**—A phagocytic cell that plays a major role in keeping the respiratory system free of microorganisms.

**Mantoux, Charles**—Formulated the Mantoux method of testing for tuberculosis which involves injecting tuberculin under the surface of the skin.

**Meerkat**—Small, insect-eating mammals native to the dry regions of Africa.

**Miliary tuberculosis**—A disseminated form of tuberculosis. The organism causes lesions to form in various parts of the body. The lesions resemble a grain called millet.

**Monocytes**—White blood cells that will ultimately develop into macrophages.

**Multiple Drug Resistant Tuberculosis (MDR-TB)**—Tuberculosis caused by tubercle bacilli that are resistant to two or more tuberculosis medications.

***Mycobacterium bovis***—Acid-fast bacilli most commonly found in cattle. The organism can cause tuberculosis in human beings.

***Mycobacterium tuberculosis***—A slender, rod-shaped, acid-fast bacterium that causes tuberculosis.

**Mycolic acid**—Large, wax-like lipids which are found in the cell walls of acid fast bacteria.

**Peptidoglycan**—A major biochemical component of all bacterial cell walls.

**Phagolysosome**—Structure which results from the fusion of the phagosome and the lysosome.

**Phagosome**—A food storage vacuole inside a phagocytic cell.

**Phthisis**—Antiquated term for tuberculosis.

**Potts Disease**—Tuberculosis of the spine.

**Purified protein derivative (PPD)**—A form of tuberculin purified by Florence Seibert in 1934. PPD is used in the Mantoux test.

**Sanatorium** (pl: **Sanatoriums**)—Special treatment facilities which housed tuberculosis patients. The sanatorium movement arose in the late 1890s and ended by the late 1950s.

**Scrofula**—Tuberculosis of the lymph nodes.

**Seibert, Florence**—Researcher who purified tuberculin in 1934, producing a product called PPD.

**Sputum**—Material coughed up from the lung.

**Streptomycin**—Antibiotic isolated by Selman Waksman and his associates in 1943. Streptomycin was the first antibiotic used to successfully treat tuberculosis.

**Superoxide dismutase**—An enzyme produced by bacteria, as well as other cells, and used to destroy toxic forms of oxygen.

**T Cell**—See **Lymphocyte**.

**TUs**—Tuberculin units. Five TUs is the standard amount injected when performing a Mantoux tuberculin skin test.

**Tine test**—A tuberculosis test which uses a multipuncture device to deliver tuberculin just below the skin.

**Trudeau, Edward**—Founder of the Saranac Lake sanatorium. Dr. Trudeau was the first person in the United States to successfully culture the tubercle bacillus.

**Tubercle**—A granuloma produced as a result of *Mycobacterium tuberculosis* infection.

**Tuberculin**—Heat-treated culture medium in which *Mycobacterium tuberculosis* was grown. Tuberculin may be used to screen patients for previous exposure to *Mycobacterium tuberculosis*.

**Virulence**—An organism's ability to cause disease.

**Waksman, Selman**—The scientist, who along with his associates, discovered and purified streptomycin in 1943.

**Wheal**—The pale, fluid-filled bubble which develops when tuberculin or PPD is injected under the skin.

# Further Reading

Alcamo, I. Edward. *Fundamentals of Microbiology*, 5th Edition. Menlo Park, Cal.: Benjamin Cummings. 1997.

Alexander, K.A., E. Pleydell, M.C. Williams, E.P. Lane, J.F.C. Nyange, and A. L. Michel. "*Mycobacterium tuberculosis*: An emerging disease of free-ranging wildlife." *Emerging Infectious Diseases* 8 (2002): 598–601.

American Thoracic Society. "Diagnostic Standards and Classification of Tuberculosis in Adults and Children." *Am J Respir Crit Care Med* 161 (2000): 1376–1395.

Berthet, F., M. Lagranderie, P. Gounon, C. Laurent-Winter, D. Ensergueix, P. Chavarot, D. Portnoi, G. Marchal, and B. Gicquel. "Attenuation of virulence by disruption of the *Mycobacterium tuberculosis erp* gene." *Science.* 282 (1998): 759-762.

Bloom, Barry R., ed. *Tuberculosis: Pathogenesis, Protection, and Control.* Washington, D.C.: ASM Press. 1994.

Bloom, Barry R., Christopher J.L. Muray. "Tuberculosis: Commentary on a Reemergent Killer." *Science.* 257 (1992): 1055–1061.

Centers for Disease Control and Prevention. "Targeted Tuberculin Testing and Treatment of Latent Tuberculosis Infection." *Mobidity and Mortality Weekly Report.* 49 (2000): 1–53.

Centers for Disease Control and Prevention. "Development of New Vaccines for Tuberculosis." *Mobidity and Mortality Weekly Report.* 47 (1998): 1–6.

Cole, S.T., R. Brosch, J. Parkhill, T. Garnier, C. Churcher, D. Harris et al. "Deciphering the biology of *Mycobacterium tuberculosis* from the complete genome sequence." *Nature.* 393 (1998): 515–516.

Cosivi, O., J.M. Grange, C.J. Daborn, M.C. Raviglioine, T. Fujikura, D. Cousins, R.A. Robinson, H.F.A.K. Huchzermeyer, I. de Kantor, and F.X. Meslin. "Zoonotic tuberculosis due to *Mycobacterium bovis* in developing countries." *Emerging Infectious Diseases.* 4 (1998): 59–70.

Cowley, G., E.A. Leonard, and M. Hager. "A Deadly Return." *Newsweek* (16 March 1992) 53–57.

Daniel, Thomas M. *Captain of Death: The Story of Tuberculosis.* Rochester, N.Y.: University of Rochester Press. 1997

Dormandy, Thomas. *The White Death, a History of Tuberculosis.* New York: New York University Press. 1999.

Dubnau, E., P. Fontan, R. Manganelli, S. Soares-Appel, and I. Smith. "*Mycobacterium tuberculosis* genes induced during infection of human macrophages." *Infection and Immunity.* 70 (2002): 2787–2795.

Dubos, R. and J. Dubos. *The White Plague: Man and Society.* New Brunswick, N.J.: Rutgers University Press. 1987.

Ezzell, Carol. "Captain of the Men of Death." *Science News* 143 (1993): 90–92.

"Focus on AIDS in New York State." New York State Department of Health AIDS Institute. (Spring 1993).

Kahn, E.A., J.R. Starke. "Diagnosis of Tuberculosis in Children: Increased Need for Better Methods." *Emerging Infectious Diseases* 1 (1995): 1–10.

Krajick, Kevin. "Floating Zoo." *Discover* (February 1997). 67–73.

Laurence, Jeffrey. "TB and AIDS: An Issue of Extraordinary Importance." *The AIDS Reader* (September/October 1992). 147–178.

Lutwick, Larry I. ed. *Tuberculosis.* London: Chapman Hall Medical. 1995

Michalak, K., C. Austin, S. Diesel, J. Maichle Bacon, and P. Zimmerman, J.N. Maslow. "*Mycobacterium tuberculosis* infection as a zoonotic disease: Transmission between humans and elephants." *Emerging Infectious Diseases.* 4 (1998): 283–287.

Reichman, Lee B., Janice Hopkins Tanne. *Timebomb, the global epidemic of multidrug resistant tuberculosis.* N.Y.: McGraw Hill. 2002.

Schlossberg, D. ed. *Tuberculosis and nontuberculosis mycobacterial infections.* Philadelphia: W.B. Saunders. 1999.

Sompayrac, Lauren. *How the Immune System Works.* Malden, Mass.: Blackwell Science Inc. 1999.

Sontag, Susan. *Illness as Metaphor.* Toronto: McGraw-Hill Ryerson Ltd., 1977.

Talaro, Kathleen P., and Arthur Talaro. *Foundations in Microbiology.* 4th edition. N.Y.: McGraw-Hill. 2002.

*Tuberculosis, a Comprehensive International Approach*, 2nd edition, Lee B. Reichman and Earl S. Hershfield eds. N.Y.: Marcel Dekker Inc. 2000.

*Tuberculosis*, W.M. Rom and S. Garay eds., N.Y.: Little Brown and Company. 1995.

Young, D.B. and B.D. Robertson. "TB Vaccines: Global Solutions for Global Problems." *Science*, 284 (1999): 1479–1480.

# Websites

Adirondack Museum Tuberculosis Information
http://www.adirondackmuseum.net/ho/tb/tbkwrd.html

American Lung Association
http://www.lungusa.org/

American Thoracic Society
http://www.thoracic.org/

Brown University TB/HIV Research Laboratory
http://www.brown.edu/Research/TB-HIV_Lab/

Centers for Disease Control, Division of Tuberculosis Elimination
http://www.cdc.gov/nchstp/tb/default.htm

Charles P. Felton National Tuberculosis Center
http://www.harlemtbcenter.org/

Francis J. Curry National Tuberculosis Center
http://www.nationaltbcenter.edu/

New Jersey Medical School National Tuberculosis Center
http://www.umdnj.edu/ntbcweb/newbldg.htm

STOP TB Homepage
http://www.stoptb.org/world.tb.day/WTBD_2002/default.asp#Background

TIGR, *Mycobacterium tuberculosis* Genome
http://www.tigr.org/tigr-scripts/CMR2/GenomePage3.spl?database=gmt

The Trudeau Institute:
http://www.trudeauinstitute.org/

Tuberculosis, Ancient Enemy, Present Threat, NAIAD
http://www.niaid.nih.gov/newsroom/focuson/tb02/tb.htm

Tuberculosis Fact Sheet NIAID
http://www.niaid.nih.gov/factsheets/tb.htm

Tuberculosis Net, the Source for Tuberculosis Teaching Materials
http://tuberculosis.net/

Tuberculosis Research Center, India
http://www.trc-chennai.org/

Tuberculosis Resources, NYC Department of Health
http://www.cpmc.columbia.edu/tbcpp/

World Health Organization Global TB Program
http://www.who.int/gtb/

# Index

Acid-fast bacillus, 80-81
Acid fast stain, 27
Aerobic organisms,
    mycobacteria as, 29
Air filtration, and HIV/
    AIDS, 95
Allergy, and tuberculin
    testing, 52
American Academy of
    Pediatrics, and Tine
    test, 56
Americas, tuberculosis in,
    14
Amikacin, 86
Ammonia, release of by
    macrophages, 47
Anergy, and tuberculin
    testing, 52
Animals, transmission of
    tuberculosis to humans
    from, 41-45
Anthrax, 18-19
Antibiotics, 22-23, 43, 60,
    70, 78-79, 80-81
    and multiple drug resis-
        tant tuberculosis,
        22-23, 68, 78, 80,
        82-84, 86, 91, 95
Appetite loss, as sign/symp-
    tom of tuberculosis, 36

Bactericidal ultra-violet
    light, and HIV/AIDS,
    95
Bavarian Alps (Germany),
    sanatoriums in, 73
BCG vaccine, 22, 37, 62-
    69
    and AIDS/HIV, 69, 95
    current production of,
        65
    effectiveness of, 66
    and high risk groups,
        68-69
    history of, 62-63
    safety of, 65

and tuberculosis
    screening test, 61
and United States, 62,
    68-69
Bloodletting, 70-71
Boosting, 60-61
Botswana, tuberculosis in
    wildlife in, 45
Bovine tuberculosis, 24,
    41-43, 45
Brehmer, Hermann, 73
Bronchoscopy, 40, 80
Brontë family, 15
    Charlotte, 8

Calmette, Albert, 62-63, 65
Caseous exudate, 34-35
Catalase, 48
Cattle, and bovine tuber-
    culosis, 24, 41-43, 45
Cause of tuberculosis
    in history, 11, 15, 16-17
    and Koch, 20
    See also Mycobacterium;
        Tuberculosis bac-
        teriu
Caves, 72
Centers for Disease Control
    and Prevention, 97
Chemical cures, 70-71
Chest X-rays, 22, 35, 43,
    51, 60
Chills, as sign/symptom
    of tuberculosis, 36
Chloride of lime, 71
Chloride of sodium, 71
Chlorine gas, 71
Chopin, Fredric, 8
Christmas Seal program,
    22
Ciprofloxacin, 86
Cohn, Ferdinand, 19
Columbus, Christopher, 14
Comprehensive TB
    Elimination Act of
    2001, 97

Consumption, 11, 36
Cord factor, 48
Cords, 24
Cost of tuberculosis, 97
Coughs
    and blood as sign/symp-
        tom of tuberculosis,
        9, 36, 60
    and transmission of
        tuberculosis, 38-39,
        51
Creosote, 71-72
Croghan, John, 72
Cytokines, 49, 50
Cytotoxic T cells, 50
    and HIV/AIDS, 90

Davos, Switzerland, sana-
    torium in, 73-74
Death, from tuberculosis,
    36
    and HIV/AIDS, 91
Defeat of tuberculosis,
    18-23
    and Koch, 16, 18-21
    and Waksman, 22-23
Delayed hypersensitivity
    reaction, 53-54
Diagnosis of tuberculosis.
    See Screening for and
    diagnosis of tubercu-
    losis
Diet, as treatment for
    tuberculosis, 11, 21,
    23, 71
Digitalis, 71
Directly observed therapy
    (DOT), 84, 86, 95
Droplet nuclei, 32
Drug susceptibility, test
    for, 80-82
Drug therapy for tuber-
    culosis, 22-23, 43, 60,
    70, 78-79, 80-82, 84,
    86-89
    and HIV/AIDS, 94-95

Ecotourism, and tuberculosis, 45
Edward I, King of England, 13
Edward IV, King of England, 8
Egypt, tuberculosis in, 8-9
Elephants, tuberculosis in, 43-45
Elixirs, 71
Ethambutol, 23, 80, 81
Europe
and BCG vaccine, 22
tuberculosis epidemic in, 13

Fatigue, as sign/symptom of tuberculosis, 36
Fevers, as sign/symptom of tuberculosis, 9, 60
Future, 97

Gaffky, Georg, 20
Galen, 11, 21, 23, 71
Genes
and search for new drugs, 87
and vaccine, 30, 66-67
Genome, of *Mycobacterium tuberculosis,* 30
Giant cells, 34
Glyoxylate shunt, 89
Goldwater Memorial Hospital (New York City), 84, 86
Gram, Christian, 26
Gram-negative bacteria, 26-27
Gram-positive bacteria, 26
Gram stain, 26
Granuloma, 48
*See also* Tubercle
Great White Death, 13

Greece, tuberculosis in, 10-11
Guafenesin, 72
Guérin, Camille, 62-63, 65

Health care workers
and BCG vaccine, 68, 69
and tuberculosis infection, 40
Hemoptysis, 9, 36
Henry VII, King of England, 13
High risk groups
and BCG vaccination, 68-69
and screening for tuberculosis, 58-59
and treatment of tuberculosis, 60
Hippocrates, 11, 70-71
History of tuberculosis, 8-17
and America, 14
and cause of tuberculosis, 11, 15, 16-17
and Egypt, 8-9
and epidemic in Europe, 13
and famous people with disease, 8, 15, 36
and Greeks, 10-11
and Middle Ages, 12-13
and Romans, 11
and romanticization, 14-15
and treatment, 11, 15, 21, 22-23, 70-77
HIV/AIDS, and tuberculosis, 23, 37, 90-97
and BCG vaccine, 69, 95
and death from tuberculosis, 91
and descriptions of HIV and AIDS, 90

and diagnosis of tuberculosis, 94
and economic and ethical concerns, 96-97
and incidence of tuberculosis, 70, 92
and latent tuberculosis, 51, 92
and multiple drug resistant tuberculosis, 91, 95
and prisons, 96
and transmission to animals, 45
and treatment, 88, 94-95
and tuberculosis testing, 52, 61, 93-94
Holliday, Doc, 8
Homeless, and HIV and tuberculosis, 95, 96
Hospitalization, for tuberculosis, 37
Hydrocyanic acid, 71
Hydrogen peroxide, release of by macrophages, 47

Immune response, 34, 46-51
and counterattack by bacterium, 48-49
and early battles, 46
and host cell arsenal, 46-47
and specific immune response, 49-50
as stalemate, 51
as unsuccessful, 51
Incidence of tuberculosis, 8, 51, 70
and HIV, 70, 92
Induration, 58, 60-61
Inflammatory reaction, to tuberculin, 53-54

Ingestion, and transmission of tuberculosis, 38-39

Inhalation, and transmission of tuberculosis, 38-39, 51

Institute for Genomic Research, The (TIGR), 30

Iodine, 71

Iron, and bacterial respiration, 47

Isocitrate lyase, 89

Isolation, and HIV/AIDS, 95

Isoniazid, 23, 79, 80, 81, 82, 95

Kaposi's sarcoma, 90

Keats, John, 8, 15

Koch, Robert, 16, 18-21, 52, 76

Koch's postulates, 20

Krebs cycle, 89

Latent tuberculosis, 35-36, 51, 89, 92

Leeuwenhoek, Anton von, 16

Leigh, Vivian, 36

Liquefaction, of tubercle, 51

Little Red, 75-76

Loeffler, Freidrich, 20

Lung hemorrhages, death from, 36

Lymph nodes, 33, 60
  and scrofula, 13

Lymphocytes, 33, 34

Lymphokines, 49
  and HIV/AIDS, 90

Lyse, 33

Lysosomes, 46-47, 48

Macrophages, 32, 34, 46-47, 48, 49, 50
  and HIV/AIDS, 90

Mammoth Cave, Kentucky, 72

Mantoux, Charles, 52-53, 58

Mantoux tests, 43, 53, 54, 56-57, 60-61, 68, 93-94

Marten, Benjamin, 16

Meerkats, tuberculosis in, 45

Middle Ages, tuberculosis in, 12-13

Miliary tuberculosis, 36

Milk, pasteurization of, 41, 42

Mongooses, tuberculosis in, 45

Monocytes, 49

Multiple drug resistant tuberculosis (MDR-TB), 22-23, 68, 78, 80, 82-84, 86, 91, 95

*Mycobacterium*, 27
  *africanum*, 24
  *bovis*, 24, 41-43
  *microti*, 24
  *tuberculosis*, 8, 14, 20, 24-30
  *See also* Tuberculosis bacterium

Mycolic acids, 25

National Institutes of Health, 97

National Tuberculosis Association, 22

Native Americans, and tuberculosis, 14

Negative pressure rooms, for health care workers, 40

New York City, directly observed therapy in, 84, 86

Night sweats, as sign/symptom of tuberculosis, 9

Ofloxacin, 86

Old tuberculin. *See* Tuberculin

Opium, 71

Organ transplant, and latent tuberculosis, 51

Oshkosh (CDC-1515), 30

Oxygen, release of by macrophages, 47, 48

Para-aminosalicylic acid (PAS), 23, 79, 86

Pasteurization, of milk, 41, 42

Pasteur, Louis, 18

Peptidoglycan, 25

Phagocytic cells, 32-33, 46-47, 53

Phagolysosome, 46-47, 48

Phagosomes, 46, 47, 48

Phthisis, 11

Pirquet, Clemens von, 52

Plato, 11

*Pneumocystis carinii*, 90
  *See also* HIV/AIDS, and tuberculosis

Poe, Edgar Allan, 8

Polyamines, release of by macrophages, 47

Potts Disease, 8-9

Prevention of tuberculosis, 37
  *See also* Vaccine

Prisons, and HIV and tuberculosis, 96

Pseudopods, 46

Purified protein derivative (PPD), 53

Pyrazinamide, 79, 80, 81

Rifabutin, 89

Rifampin, 23, 79, 80, 81, 82, 89, 95

Rifapentine, 89

Romanticization of tuberculosis, 14-15

Rome, tuberculosis in, 11
Roosevelt, Eleanor, 8

Saint Säens, Camille, 14-15
Sanatoriums, 15, 23, 73-77
Sanger Centre, 30
Saranac Lake, New York,
    sanatorium in, 15, 75-
    76
Screening and diagnosis
    for tuberculosis, 22, 52
    and AIDS/HIV
    patients, 52, 61, 93-
    94
    and BCG vaccine, 61
    and complications
    and drawbacks of
    testing, 60-61
    in high risk groups,
    58-59
    and Mantoux test, 43,
    53, 54, 56-57, 60-61,
    68, 93-94
    and purified protein
    derivative, 53
    and reaction at inocu-
    lation site, 53-54,
    55, 58-59
    and signs and symp-
    toms of tuberculo-
    sis, 9, 36, 60
    and Tine test, 54-56
    and tuberculin, 20-21,
    52-57
    and X-rays, 22, 35, 43,
    51, 60
Scrofula, 13, 41
Seibert, Florence, 53
Shakespeare, William, 13
Shelly, Percy, 15
Signs and symptoms of
    tuberculosis, 9, 36, 60
Sneezes, and transmission
    of tuberculosis, 38-39
Specific immune response,
    49-50

Sputum, 22
    bloody, 9, 36
    cultures of, 60
Steroid therapy for
    arthritis, and latent
    tuberculosis, 51
Stevenson, Robert Louis,
    15
Streptomycin, 22-23, 78,
    79
Superoxide dismutase, 48
Switzerland, sanatorium
    in, 73-74

T cells, 49-50, 53, 90
Thiacetazone, 86
Thionamide, 86
Thoreau, Henry David, 8
Tine test, 54-56
T lymphocytes, and
    HIV/AIDS, 90, 92
Transmission of tubercu-
    losis, 32, 37, 38-45
    from animals to
    humans, 41-45
    and health care workers,
    40
    and inhalation/inges-
    tion from coughs
    and sneezes, 38-39,
    51
    prevention of, 37
    and susceptibility, 37,
    44-45
Treatment of tuberculosis,
    70-89
    and antibiotics, 22-23,
    43, 60, 70, 78-79,
    80-81
    and bloodletting, 70-
    71
    and caves, 72
    and chemical cures,
    71-72
    and directly observed
    therapy, 84, 86, 95

    and drug susceptibility,
    80-82
    and drug therapy, 22-
    23, 43, 60, 70, 78-79,
    80-82, 84, 86-89,
    94-95
    and elixirs, 71
    and genes, 30
    in high risk group, 60
    in history, 11, 15, 21,
    22-23, 70-77
    and HIV/AIDS, 88,
    94-95
    at home, 37
    and hospitalization,
    37
    and multiple drug
    resistant tubercu-
    losis, 22-23, 68, 78,
    80, 82-84, 86, 91,
    95
    and nutritional diet,
    11, 21, 23, 71
    and sanatoriums, 23,
    73-77
    and search for new
    drugs, 87-89
    and tuberculosis
    infection, 82
    See also Antibiotics
Trudeau, Edward Living-
    ston, 15, 74-76
Trudeau Institute at
    Saranac Lake, 76
Trudeau School for
    Tuberculosis, 76
Tubercle, 34-35, 36, 48-
    49
    liquefaction of, 51
Tuberculin (old tuber-
    culin), 20-21, 52-57
    See also Screening for
    and diagnosis of
    tuberculosis
Tuberculosis association,
    first, 22

Tuberculosis bacterium,
24-31
characteristics of in
culture, 27, 28
early knowledge of,
16-17
genetics of, 30
physical characteristics
of, 24-25
staining characteristics
of, 26-27
Tuberculosis disease, 36-
37, 37
Tuberculosis infection,
25, 32-36, 37, 82
Tuberculosis research,
future of, 97

United States
and BCG vaccine, 62,
68-69
cost of tuberculosis in,
97
sanatorium movement
in, 74-75
tuberculosis research
in, 97

Vaccine
and genes, 30, 66-67
and Koch, 20-21
search for new, 66-67
See also BCG vaccine
Villemin, Jean-Antoine,
16-17

Virchow, Rudolf, 15
Virulence, 24, 25, 66

Waksman, Selman, 22-23
Weakness, as sign/symptom
of tuberculosis, 36
Weight loss/wasting, as
sign/symptom of tuber-
culosis, 9, 36, 60
Wheal, 57
World Health Organization
and directly observed
therapy, 86
and tuberculosis and
HIV, 92

X-rays, 35, 43, 51, 60

# Picture Credits

9: Courtesy WHO
10: NMHM, Armed Forces Institute of Pathology
12: National Library of Medicine
19: © The Nobel Foundation
23: Waksman Foundation for Microbiology
29: Courtesy Center for Tuberculosis Research, Johns Hopkins University
33: ©Lester V. Bergman/Corbis
35: ©Lester V. Bergman/Corbis
39: ©Bettmann/Corbis
42: CDC, Emerging Infectious Diseases
44: ©Peter Chadwick; Gallo Image/Corbis
47: Courtesy Center for Tuberculosis Research, Johns Hopkins University
49: Lambda Science Artwork
55: Lambda Science Artwork
57: Lambda Science Artwork
59: Courtesy CDC
64: ©Bettmann/Corbis
74: Courtesy of The Adirondack Museum
75: Courtesy of The Adirondack Museum
77: © Bettmann/Corbis
81: Courtesy CDC
83: Courtesy CDC
87: Courtesy WHO
92: Courtesy WHO

Cover: Courtesy CDC

# About the Author

Kim R. Finer received her B.A. in microbiology at Miami University and her Ph.D. in veterinary microbiology at Texas A&M University. She currently is an associate professor in the Department of Biological Sciences at Kent State University where she teaches courses in microbiology, human genetics, and ecology. She has written textbooks on the use of internet resources in the classroom and has published numerous papers in the areas of biology education as well as in her research area. She received the Exxon Foundation Innovation in Education Award in 1996 and was elected to Who's Who Among America's Teachers in 1998. Kim was also recently identified as a national model course developer by the SENCER program of the Association of American Colleges and Universities. She lives in Wooster, Ohio, with her two teenage children, Ben and Julia, her husband John, and dog Jenny.

# About the Editor

The late I. Edward Alcamo was a Distinguished Teaching Professor of Microbiology at the State University of New York at Farmingdale. Alcamo studied biology at Iona College in New York and earned his M.S. and Ph.D. degrees in microbiology at St. John's University, also in New York. He taught at Farmingdale for over 30 years. In 2000, Alcamo won the Carski Award for Distinguished Teaching in Microbiology, the highest honor for microbiology teachers in the United States. He was a member of the American Society for Microbiology, the National Association of Biology Teachers, and the American Medical Writers Association. Alcamo authored numerous books on the subjects of microbiology, AIDS, and DNA technology as well as the award-winning textbook *Fundamentals of Microbiology*, now in its sixth edition.

# DATE DUE

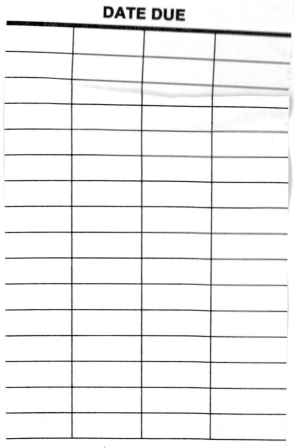

The Library Store   #47-0103